Everything I know about Leadership
I learnt from the Kids

Everything I know about Leadership I learnt from the Kids

KEITH COATS

PENGUIN BOOKS

PENGUIN BOOKS

Published By the Penguin Group
80 Strand, London WC2R 0RL, England
Penguin Putnam Inc, 375 Hudson Street, New York, New York 10014,
USA
Penguin Books Australia Ltd, 250 Camberwell Road, Camberwell,
Victoria 3124, Australia
Penguin Books Canada Ltd, 10 Alcorn Avenue, Toronto, Ontario,
Canada M4V 3B2
Penguin Books (NZ) Ltd, Cnr Rosedale and Airborne Roads, Albany,
Auckland, New Zealand
Penguin Books India (Pvt) Ltd, 11 Community Centre, Panscheel Park,
New Delhi – 110 017, India
Penguin Books (South Africa) (Pty) Ltd, 24 Sturdee Avenue, Rosebank,
Johannesburg 2196, South Africa

Penguin Books (South Africa) (Pty) Ltd, Registered Offices:
24 Sturdee Avenue, Rosebank, Johannesburg 2196, South Africa

First published by Penguin Books (South Africa) (Pty) Ltd 2005

ISBN 0 143 02457 4

Typeset by CJH Design in 11 on 15pt Century
Cover design: Flame Design, Cape Town
Printed and bound by Creda Communications

During the editing process, I received the following note from my editor:

You are hard on Vicky! Can I ask whether she's completely OK with it? I'm sure she must be, but feel duty bound to ask the question
… and of course she has a point!

So it is only fitting and entirely appropriate that I dedicate this book to my wonderful (and long-suffering) wife Vicky, without whom this book simply would not have been possible. She is our family's mainstay and superglue.

I love you, Vicky.

Then there are the kids (ours and others') who have been my teachers as I have been allowed to participate in their magical world.
'Ah Dad, no way! You can't include that story!' was a frequent response by one or more of the kids to my enthusiastic rendition of yet another completed chapter.
So, special thanks to them – even if they do follow through with their threat to change their surname and emigrate.

Then there have been those like Jenny and Graeme, among others, who have constantly encouraged me to share my stories with a wider (and unsuspecting) public.
Thank you all.

Now, where did I leave that passport and ticket? And where the heck is Borneo anyway?

Acknowledgements

The author and publisher gratefully acknowledge the following persons and instances for permission to quote from copyright material:

Simon & Schuster Inc ('The Velveteen Rabbit', *The Book of Virtues* by William J Bennett); HarperCollins Publishers Ltd (*Does God Have a Big Toe?* By Rabbi Marc Gellman); Margaret Wheatley for extracts from *Leadership and the New Science* (BK Publishers, San Francisco, 1999); Leonard Sweet (*Quantum Spirituality*, Whaleprints, Dayton, Ohio, 1991); McGraw Hill (*The Dream Society* by Rolf Jensen, 1999).

Every effort has been made to trace copyright holders or their assigns. The author and publisher apologise for any inadvertent infringement of copyright and will be pleased to include acknowledgement in any future editions if this is drawn to their attention.

Contents

Introduction

And to think that I saw it on Mulberry Street

I will never forget the emotions that accompanied holding my firstborn, a son, in my arms for the very first time. I felt so proud. Well, actually, I felt so clever, like I had achieved this amazing feat all on my own – an illusion that was quickly dispelled and something which I have now come to accept I had very little to do with, according to my wife's epic version of the childbearing and birthing process.

I remember thinking how much he looked like Winston Churchill ... not a popular observation, I might add, with the assembled and somewhat biased admirers. This experience taught me to keep such spontaneous observations to myself, and never more so than when observing the infants of other doting parents who just don't seem to see the prune-like qualities most babies arrive with. What I didn't know at that memorable time, however, was just how much I would learn about life from that bundle in my arms. Of course the first bundle was soon followed by a second and eventually by a third ... slow to learn, I can hear you thinking, and in some respects you would be right.

Naturally, life was never to be the same again.

My wife Vicky and I have gone through the respective life cycles that mark the hazardous terrain we call 'parenting'. The 2am feedings that turn into 2am dates; the fear that one day these precious little beings (or 'Sacred Beings' as the Sioux refer to them) will grow up and leave home, morphing into the very real fear that they will never leave home; the worry that they won't complete their schooling becoming the panic that they will want to go to university, further stretching my financial enslavement; the 'look how cute they are together', to 'touch my daughter and I'll hang you out to dry'. Sure there are others, but I think you get my point.

As I watched these Sacred Beings that inhabited our home grow up there was a growing awareness of just how valuable they were in pointing me to fresh life lessons; in particular, lessons about leadership.

A lot has been said and written about leadership and not much of it, I suspect, is very new. Seldom has a subject been rehashed, reworded, re-engineered, remodelled, reworked and re-everything as this age-old preoccupation with leadership. But there you have it, and I will certainly not be the one to provide the final or authoritative word on the subject. In fact, providing 'the final word' is not possible because leadership, like life, can never be fixed, static or unchanging. If leadership is to be appropriate it has to be contextual, and so it is with parenting.

As I have read about leadership, studied it, practised it and even in a sense made a living out of it, what I have noticed is one amazing trend: the most enduringly popular books on business topics are the most simple. Certainly the 'One Minute Manager' series by Ken Blanchard got the ball rolling and the most recent example would be the almost inexplicable success of *Who moved my Cheese?* (which I might add fails to provide the answer to the question posed by the title). The fact that the cheese book comes a distant second in comprehension ability to most of the books on any ten-year-old child's bookshelf, including Harry Potter, makes you wonder about adults, comprehension and leadership.

So what is it about business leaders who would prefer to read the simple books but who nonetheless stack some of the more respectable titles on their shelves? Closer scrutiny invariably reveals unmarked pages and a layer of dust, dead giveaways concerning the reading and application of such resources.

I suspect that most leaders simply don't have the time or inclination to wade through volumes of uninspiring theory and knee-deep research. Most are looking for easy to understand, easy to identify with and easy to implement suggestions, ideas and 'aha' type truths.

In other words, stories.

Stories seem to have an innate ability to inspire and live with the reader in much the same way as that comfortable old jacket or favourite pair of shoes. Stories can emerge out of the natural ingredients of daily life or be cobbled together with make-believe ingredients from magical worlds embedded in the imagination, but either way they have the ability to connect, transport and surround one in an almost mystical way.

And this is where the kids come in.

These lab rats (no offence, you lot) have provided me, and I hope you (by the time you have finished reading this offering), a real time case study in the art of corporate leadership. Most, but not all, of the stories I write about emanate from our particular cave. However, irrespective of the cave from which they come, all the stories have their gravitational centre rooted firmly in the world of kids.

Perhaps our adult world is not all that different from that of a kindergarten. As we recognise the need to infuse fun, adventure and play into our all too serious settings, we could learn a thing or two from kids everywhere, the undisputed kings (and queens) of the playground.

During the time that I have had the privilege of participating in the unfinished business of parenting (does it ever end?) some incredible truths have emerged as I have thought about leadership.

It has been said that it is important to learn from the mistakes of others – because you won't live long enough to make them all yourself. This book, then, has been written to share a bundle of insights, reflections and mistakes with you. I am sure that you could add several of your own. I am also sure that those of you who have been called upon to be a parent will be able to relate in your own unique way to what I have written.

I have even decided to share stories that some might argue should not be allowed to see the light of day, or at the very least not pass beyond the portals of the Coats household. So I apologise in advance to those who have provided me with subject matter for the book and assure them that names and places have *not* been changed to protect their identity. I have greatly enjoyed rummaging and scratching around the memory loft in search of these stories. Some have been easy to find, others less so. But once located, dusted off and stacked in a pile, they have shone brightly, yielding, I believe, some wonderful lessons for those who serve others through their leadership.

I hope you will enjoy what is on offer and that reading this book will awaken your own treasure chest of memories which, as they yawn and stretch themselves, will bring lightness, humour and effectiveness into your own leadership context.

Such are the unfolding lessons we learn from those whom we have the wonderful responsibility to teach, lead, and give our hard earned money to … our kids!

Scribblings ...

It was the Irish poet and scholar John O'Donohue who wrote, '*You travelled a great distance to get here*', and French philosopher Blaise Pascal who bestowed on us the phrase, '*We are embarked*'. Indeed, we have already travelled some way to get where we are today and yet we still find ourselves embarking on new voyages of discovery. I invite you to take off those shoes and socks, and enjoy both the memories and the journey ...

Theodore Geisel's first book was rejected by twenty-three publishers before it was finally accepted and went on to sell millions of copies, as did all his other books. 'Who was Theodore Geisel?' you ask. None other than Dr Seuss. And that first book? *And to think that I saw it on Mulberry Street.*

'The only "ordinary" homes seem to be the ones we don't know much about.'

– C S Lewis

(*Letters to an American Lady*, Grand Rapids, Mich, William B. Eerdman, 1967, p44)

'Leadership, an amorphous phenomenon that has intrigued us since people began organizing, is being examined now for its relational aspects. Few if any theorists ignore the complexity of relationships that contribute to a leader's effectiveness. Instead, there are more and more studies on partnership, followership, empowerment, teams, networks, and the role of context.'

– Margaret Wheatley

(*Leadership and the New Science*, BK Publishers, San Francisco, 1999)

I'm six now

The importance of celebrating and remembering

'I'm six now,' were the first words to greet me on the morning of 1 December (a nice change from the usual rasping, 'Coffee', from the semi-comatose form lying next to me). It was also the first morning in six that the sun had shown itself; a nice touch, I thought, and somewhat appropriate for Sipho's birthday.

Six years is a momentous milestone. It heralds the first of many years spent in formal education – a process where the kid gets smarter and the parents poorer. In Sipho's case it is also marked by the acquisition of his own set of wheels and will become the year of mastering the skills that will help keep him on top of them, not under them. Though the tough part is knowing that the latter invariably precedes the former. Still, it is a skill that lasts a lifetime, as demonstrated by a ninety-year-old riding her bicycle around Scotland and featured on some late night travel programme I happened to watch a few days ago.

It will be the only year that he attends the same school as both his older brother and sister (spare a thought for the teaching staff, won't you). It will be the time he learns all those important six-year-old-type things that, stacked together, reveal further glimpses of the life being shaped before our very eyes. An awesome process indeed, and every parent of a six-year-old will know exactly what I am talking about.

It doesn't seem six years ago that as a family we sat on the lawn of a children's home laying siege to a tiny baby on a blanket. I had come directly from a bus that had transported sixty rowdy young people home from a youth camp. I was tired but elated to be meeting our 'new' son. Our adoption application had been in process for several months and finally we were nearing the end or, I guess, actually the beginning. As we sat on the lawn the social worker repeatedly asked us, 'Do you like him?' A strange question, I remember thinking at the time.

It wasn't difficult to settle on the name 'Sipho' (which means 'Gift' in Zulu) and somehow 'Daniel' tagged along bringing with it the heroic aura of the Daniel of old who got to share a room with some lions.

So Daniel Sipho arrived and suddenly the theory of adoption gave way to the practical. There were many moments in those early years when we wished we could just freeze the frame – except of course for the nappies! There were many and often humorous encounters with curious strangers who more often than not proved to be generous in their on-the-spot support, encouragement and, on one occasion, loud prayers. We in turn had to find a way to explain 'adoption', as there is no Zulu word for a concept that is unknown.

In both name and presence Sipho is a gift to those who inhabit the Coats household. People have often said to us, 'Sipho is such a fortunate little boy.' They really don't understand. It is the other tribe members who are the fortunate ones. At a number of points the adoption process brings you face to face with your most basic values and motivations. What a gift that is!

Leaders often fail to see the 'gift' embedded in situations and processes that invite inspection of our basic values and motivations. These situations may be those tough or unusual circumstances where the temptation to avoid altogether or take a wide detour is strong. However, they may also be one of those frequent opportunities along life's journey that give us the chance to pause at a milestone, celebrate and reflect on the journey already travelled as well as the one that lies ahead. All too often we readily apply ourselves and the resources at our disposal to the 'what?' 'how?' and 'when?' type questions – the practical stuff – for after all they are the ones which keep us busy and looking productive.

But it is the 'why?' question we neglect.

Perhaps we started out with it but then over the long haul it faded into the disappearing horizon and we think that having entertained it once means that we never have to return to its demanding scrutiny. We need to take the time to revisit the 'why?'. It takes us to the very core of things and, once there, we must be prepared to accept that we will not always find answers, and sometimes just be content that we are in that space, content to have found a clearing in the thicket of schedules, activities and busyness that surround us. It is that 'pause space' which gives us the gift of exhilarating, perhaps scary, opportunities to recreate and discover new beginnings.

Celebrate the milestones but remember the beginnings. And don't neglect to look out for the 'gifts' that life puts in our path – they invite discovery!

Scribblings ...

Before Christmas every year it has become a family tradition to agree on something for which we as a family are grateful, something that has taken place during the course of the about-to-be-discarded year. That decided, we fashion a Christmas decoration that will hang from our tree and come to symbolise whatever it is we have decided to celebrate and remember. It does mean that we have some pretty bizarre tree decorations (a cricket bat, a plane, a trophy and even, on one occasion, some carpeting!). But each year as we decorate the tree we take time to remember and celebrate. Of course it also provides a great conversation piece to counter the quizzical stares that eventually erupt with comments such as, 'That's an interesting tree you have there ...' that are really thinly disguised questions inviting an explanation.

And who's to say that this can't be done within the context of the office?

You can call me Mr Coats

Leadership: a doubting kind of faith

'You can call me Mr Coats,' was the emphatic reply given by one Sipho Coats aged five to 'Lochie' (abbreviation for 'Loch Ness Monster' ie Vicky's mom). All this transpired during a telephone conversation which centred on why Lochie called him 'Daniel', his first name, and not 'Sipho', his more common zip code.

'Mr Coats' was going through a stage where almost every sentence began with a 'why?' 'where?' 'what?' or 'how?' This reduced his demented mother to the 'Aauurgh' stage, which I somehow don't think is Gaelic for 'bless you, my precious' – but then again, I've been wrong before.

Questions are important though.

Recently I heard it said that the 'opposite of faith is

certainty'. I like that. In fact the more I have thought about it the more I have come to realise that a faith that fails to embrace our doubts and questions is perhaps not much of a faith at all. To others, faith needs to be somewhat barred and guarded, surrounded by high walls, closed, grim and rather unattractive.

Os Guinness writes that 'to understand doubt is to have a key to a quiet heart and quiet mind'. I wonder, then, if the faith needed for leadership today is one that ought to incorporate vulnerability, a faith made strong by embracing our questions and doubts rather than one stuffed with answers and certainty. A faith without walls.

What would such leadership look like? Whatever its appearance, I suspect the world could do with more of this brand of leadership.

Faith and leadership are not common bedfellows in the volumes written from a leadership perspective. But the two cannot be divorced and the smart leader knows that they are intrinsically linked.

I have encountered two basic constructs of faith (whatever that faith may be) which can often imprint on the leadership philosophy and style of the carrier. A picture will explain what I am getting at here:

For some, faith is like a shop window display where everything is deliberately and carefully chosen. The items selected are just the right size and are meticulously colour coordinated. The overall design aims to arrest the attention of passers-by with the intention of attracting them into the shop to purchase what they have seen in the window. The display sets out to be attractive and inviting, but is clearly not to be messed or tampered with in any way. There are those for whom faith is assembled in this manner. Things are structured and in place, and in no need of rearranging. No questions are asked, other than how to acquire the items in order to replicate the window display.

Then there are others for whom faith is more like a wide-open barn door. To those walking past (off the beaten track, I imagine, as I haven't seen too many barns in Main Street which means that passers-by are usually exploring or lost or both), the invitation is to enter and observe the activity taking place in the barn. A newly made table here, a broken chair there; sawdust, scattered pieces of timber and off-cuts and the sounds of sawing, sanding and hammering together with the distinctive smell of freshly cut wood and drying varnish. Work is in progress, items are at various stages of completion, from drawings pinned on the walls to boxes packed and ready to go. Evidence of failure as well as success greets visitors who stick their noses through the wide-open doors, attracted by the sounds, curious to explore, or perhaps ask for directions or even shelter from the elements. In the barn faith is about a process, a journey ... fewer answers and more questions; less design and more experimentation.

The question then becomes: Is your leadership more like the shop window ... or the barn?

Scribblings ...

'Far better an approximate answer to the right question which is often vague, than an exact answer to the wrong question which can always be made precise.'

— John Tukey, Statistician

Arianna asked: 'Mommy, I have a big toe, and you have a big toe, and Daddy has a big toe. Does God have a big toe too?'

— Rabbi Marc Gellman

(*Does God Have a Big Toe?* New York, Harper & Row, 1989, p43)

'Faith is not simply intellectual understanding, or an act of human intention, or following some salvation "how-to" manual, or assent to creedal formulations. Faith is not a matter of doing, or even being, but an experience of becoming. Experiencing is faith's most fundamental activity.'

— Leonard I Sweet

(*Quantum Spirituality*, Whaleprints, Dayton, OH, 1991, p69)

Acknowledgement: Os Guinness, *Doubt* published by Lion Publishing Corporation, Albatross Books Pty Ltd. First published under the title *In Two Minds* (1976). The phrase quoted on page 13 appears on the cover as a subtitle.

Dopey and Speed: Hamsters with short (but fulfilled) lives

Life is seasonal

Let me start at the beginning. Some time ago I arrived home to be greeted by Tamryn's: 'Dad, can I please have a horse?' I remember being asked a similar question by her older brother once, though if my memory serves me correctly it was a kangaroo that he wanted. In his case a 'Sure boy, when you turn thirty-five', appeased the gods and seemed a real win-win solution. However I didn't think I would escape so easily this time round – not when I looked into my daughter's imploring brown eyes.

Anyway after some tough, no holds barred negotiations we compromise by settling on two hamsters. I find out later that the 'horse ploy' is a well practised tactic in the parent manipulation psychology of: If you want a hamster, start out by asking for a horse. So along with the dogs, cats, birds and fish, Noah's ark adds two hamsters and I look into the legalities of changing my name to Dr Doolittle.

The hamsters arrive home following very little deliberation as to which ones to choose when we are confronted by the overcrowded cage at the pet store. This only confirms my earlier suspicions of the entire thing being a set-up and the 'win-win' takes on a 'win-hopelessly outclassed' type of character.

Appropriately named 'Dopey' and 'Speed', these mouse-like creatures soon have us on a treadmill. Dopey gets tangled up on the wheel which results in an ER situation. No sooner has that been resolved than he goes AWOL (Absent Without Official Leave). The mother of all hamster hunts takes place with the Director (this time me) encouraging the troops to 'think like a hamster' in order to find our furry friend – a strategic tactic I learnt while watching a late night action movie. (I've always told Vicky that these movies have merit.) No sooner has this battle command gone out than mom finds Dopey ... enough said! Glancing over my shoulder as I write this Vicky, seeing the 'mom finds Dopey' bit, adds a rather caustic, 'Writing about us again are you, love?' (This must be one of the reasons that the good B-grade action movies are scheduled late at night away from those who simply don't understand their intricate plots and appreciate the true depth of their character portrayals.) As she leaves the room, I make a mental note to shift my writing habits to a late night slot.

The wild celebrations centring on our Pet Detective after the recapture of Dopey are curtailed by Dopey's untimely demise a couple of days later. It turns out that Sipho dropped him, thereby ending not only Dopey's short but happy existence but Sipho's future in any courier business. This whole episode put understandable strain on sister-brother relationships, resulting in our own Truth and Reconciliation Commission. However, peace was soon restored and the burial service, a solemn affair, was attended only by immediate family.

We have seen many pets come and go, with cats somehow having the shortest life expectancy. (Vicky was once known as the 'Butcher of Caversham' for her effortless talent for riding over these hapless animals. The fact that cats are amongst the most agile creatures on our planet only serves to increase one's appreciation of Vicky's driving skills!)

The point is, life is seasonal. Leaders would do well to remember this truth and lead and live according to this law of life. (That and keeping clear of Vicky's tailgate!)

To be conscious of the seasons is to be an observer of life. For some this is natural, part of who they are; for other it requires a conscious effort and discipline. I recall a friend who had grown up on a farm in South Africa telling me of a conversation she had once had with one of the farm labourers, an old Zulu man. She had paused to admire the stunning African sunset but her action and comments drew a blank with the old man. For him, appreciating the daily miracle of the African sunset was inbuilt; it did not need special reflection and attention. It was simply part and parcel of his world view.

Seasonal changes bring all kinds of adjustments. Not to make the necessary adjustments, especially in more extreme climates would be foolhardy. Yet so often leaders fail to apply this logic to their own 'seasonal changes' and transitions.

I once sat with the CEO of one of the most successful franchises in South African history, hearing of the adventure that the company had embarked on ten years earlier that had seen them accomplish spectacular growth and success. However, he reflected, their success had all the signs of having now reached a plateau and even, in his opinion, was showing the first stages of decline. Something was urgently needed to relaunch, to kick-start a new growth curve. He recounted repeated attempts to initiate innovative steps that would achieve the desired results, but each had gone only so far before retreat to the safety of the known and the comfortable occurred. He spoke of a leadership team (one with a ten-year history) that led from memory rather than towards innovation. The eventual outcome had been to dismiss the entire team in order to launch something new.

This is indicative of the harsh reality that many leaders, well schooled in a modern, mechanistic, industrial-age world, are facing. We are right now in the transition period from modern to postmodern, from the information economy to the relational or connection economy. Leading from memory will not, *cannot*, work.

My friend Meg Wheatley put it well when she wrote: 'I like to think of (what I do) as reminiscent of the early chart books used by explorers sailing in search of new lands. Those early maps and accompanying commentary were descriptive but not predictive, enticing but not fully revelatory. They pointed in certain directions, illuminated landmarks, warned of dangers, yet their elusive references and blank spaces served to encourage explorations and discoveries by other people. They contained colourful embellishments of areas and events that had struck the wanderer's fancy and ignored other important places. They contained life-saving knowledge, passed hand to hand among those who were willing to dare similar voyages of their own.' (*Leadership and the New Science*, Preface, p xiii).

Clearly it is time for some leaders to recognise and adapt to prevailing seasonal changes.

Scribblings ...

Hernán Cortés was one of the conquerors in the age of sea exploration – a ruthless man who virtually destroyed the Aztec empire. He was charged by the King of Spain to conquer the Aztec empire of Montezuma, in modern day Mexico. He set sail with a small, dedicated crew. The voyage was arduous and rough, and there were many skirmishes with pirates, local inhabitants and even their own countrymen. But eventually, in 1519, the small and demoralised force arrived on the shores of Vera Cruz. Cortés realised that his men were not as committed to the goal as they should have been. Making landfall, he sent the crew to forage for food and water. While they were away, he issued his now legendary command … 'Burn the boats!'

No longer could his men entertain thoughts of returning home. No longer was the option of looking back available. They had entered the new land, with all its challenges, dangers and opportunities. Now they had to understand it, survive, and even thrive in it – or die trying.

There was no going back. The boats were burned.

Like the explorers in the age of discovery, we have lived through a time of extraordinary advances in communication technologies, among many other areas, and the world is a much smaller place than it used to be. The telephone, computers, cellphones, satellites, television and, most recently, the Internet, have transformed and reconfigured the world. And that is only the beginning!

A new age of discovery has dawned, and we are the bold navigators, heading out to unknown shores. Like Cortés, we find that people are nervous and unhappy. They long for the comfort of the past. We need to step boldly into the new land of the twenty-first century and choose to understand it, survive and even thrive in it.

The challenge is not only to envisage and understand the context for tomorrow's leadership, but to be found standing courageously where it meets today.

Eyes wide shut: Seeing the lion

Visionary leadership

'It's your turn,' accompanied by a rib-breaking jab to my side proved to be a firm deterrent to any further sleep and left me in no doubt that to protest would be about as successful as Custer's last stand. Arising from the fog of coma-like slumber when all the sane world is sleeping is never easy but the fact that I did so was aided by the knowledge that unless rapid progress was made towards this end, further collateral damage could be expected.

As my mind and body desperately tried to find each other I locked on to the source of this intrusion into my sleep: Keegan's cries of 'Daddy, Daddy' were as unmistakable as they were persistent. As I made my way to his room I wondered just how to ensure that in the future night calls could be rewired to 'Mommy, Mommy' and 'Daddy, Daddy' reserved for daylight saving only. Programming this kind of software into kids could make me a hero, a *rich* hero, to millions of fathers all around the world, I thought to myself; I would become a legend amongst men. Arrival at my destination curtailed any further development of this line of thought, but I promised myself that I would revisit this potentially ingenious idea.

'Daddy, there's a lion in my room,' were the words that greeted me as I popped my head around the door and instantly I understood why it was I who had been called to duty. Lion-tamer, Superdad – a life-threatening situation that required the bravest of the brave ... a job for dad! An exhaustive search ensued, one that Keegan watched wide-eyed from the safety of his bed, interrupting me from time to time to offer suggestions that had me looking in places where no self-respecting man-eater would choose to hide – a pencil case for one.

Eventually, the search concluded, I submitted my 'no lion' report to a clearly doubtful client and turned to leave the room to return to the sleep that I had left behind. It was as I turned off the light that I heard Keegan mutter to himself, *'Of course there is a lion here. I see him every time I close my eyes.'*

Seeing what others see when they close their eyes is something leaders who know how to inspire vision and nurture dreamers need to be able to do.

Organisations need dreamers, the fringe thinkers, the people who see things others don't. It often happens that such people are not an easy fit in organisations and one is tempted to wish life without them. In his book *Maverick* Ricardo Semler writes that every company should be paying someone to be looking out the window. To be taking in the big picture, to be surveying the landscape, to be dreaming of what could be. Leaders are often under pressure to be this person, the person with their eyes wide shut. While this isn't necessarily the best place for leaders, you do need to ensure that someone is doing this and when their report is given and the lion is spotted, the leader needs to be the one who declares loudly and clearly, 'Well, why not?'

Such leaders are often called visionaries.

(Ricardo Semler, *Maverick*, Century, London, 1993)

Scribblings ...

In his book *The Dream Society* Rolf Jensen talks about planning for the future as being 'fiction with no plot'.

'Businesses need to imagine their futures, the way good novelists imagine their stories. George Simenon, the renowned Belgian writer of detective stories, is a fine storyteller capable of evoking images of Paris through his descriptions of sounds, music, dance halls and bistros. When you read his books it's like being there yourself. He is a master of the *mise en scène* with all its props and backdrops. He also makes his characters exude mystery right to the very last page. Similarly, business scenarios are a stage and the market is the play with its actors. The futurist sets the stage for the play that will unfold in the market of the future. That the word "scenario" is etymologically related to "scene" is no wonder. The scenario is the background for the drama of the market. Operating with scenarios makes it easier to answer companies' questions about the future: what stage are we to act on, what does the scenery look like, what colour is the backdrop? In science fiction, the scenery is often the most important ingredient; describing the distant future is more important than the plot – except of course in good science fiction. The Star Wars saga is both a description of an alien galaxy whose civilizations are battling – a brilliant scenario – and also a heart-rending myth about the victory of good over evil.

'The comparison of scenario planning to the world of theatre and fiction is no accident. Building scenarios is not merely an analytic exercise, a stringent and technical process. It is also part drama and part dream. The future demands that you manage uncertainty, and the scenarios are the proper tools – alternative visualizations of the market in 3 to 5 years, in 5 to 10 years.'

(*The Dream Society*, McGraw-Hill, New York, 1999, pp27-8)

Naming body parts

Leadership and diversity

I remember once reading that middle-age happens when you keep thinking that in a couple of weeks you'll be back to normal.

To be honest I am not sure that I am clear as to exactly what constitutes 'normality' – or at least if I once was, I no longer am. This applies particularly when I hear Vicky's mom say, 'Why can't everyone just be normal like me?'

Perhaps any home inhabited by junior tribe members sooner or later has to discard the 'normal' tag. Well, if they're honest they do. How else do you explain the bold, matter of fact announcement of one Sipho Coats that he had named a certain part of his anatomy, which, I hasten to add, I'll refrain from mentioning explicitly in this suitable-for-all-ages story.

'Given your *WHAT* a name?' was mom's shrill reaction which was quickly balanced by my more composed, 'That's interesting, son, what is your … er … um … ah's name?'

'Free Willy 2,' came the reply.

Stunned non-comprehension was followed by much hilarity, something clearly not understood by the proud owner of Free Willy 2.

Despite protestations, backed-up by solid research, that this sort of behaviour was considered normal within the male species of the tribe, all attempts to secure mainstream recognition for the practice failed.

All of which brings me to the point of asking: What is normal? Certainly in today's world, and increasingly in tomorrow's world, 'normal' is an ever-shrinking concept as tolerance for diversity and globalisation increase. Leading from the presumption that others will see and interpret things the way you do and share your world view, is a sure recipe for failure. Skilled leaders are those who are able to lead in the midst of diversity.

As people increasingly resist the melting pot of the 'one-culture-fits-all' mentality, leaders will be required to learn and live by a different set of rules and embrace new skills for twenty-first century leadership.

For most leaders this will not be a walk in the park. But failure to make such adjustments will ensure that one loses touch with those one leads – and perhaps there can be no more serious failure of leadership than that reality.

Scribblings ...

The problem with innovation is that it requires the leader to embrace diversity. And that in turn leads to further challenges for the leader since diversity, if it is to flourish, needs the air of a democratic environment. Democracy for most leaders looks messy, out of control and something to be avoided. A degree of 'participative management', yes, but democracy ... well, how long have you been smoking those socks? 'It will never work and it is way too risky even to attempt to travel this road' about sums up the more polite responses.

But it can work, as Richardo Semler, the avant-garde Brazilian CEO of Semco, has so aptly demonstrated. His two books *Maverick* and the more recent *The Seven Day Weekend* (certainly an attractive title!) are well worth reading. This is no academic from Harvard who theorises in the middle-earth realm of business leadership spouting heresies, but rather someone, much like you perhaps, who is engaged in the reality of everyday leadership and running a business.

It is possible to develop the kind of environment where diversity thrives and makes innovation possible. The problem is that in order to take this road less travelled we have to unlearn and deconstruct much of what we have gathered about leadership during the journey. Semler offers some practical points of departure for changing direction on this journey which, in his experience at least, have resulted in some amazing outcomes.

Not long ago I was chatting to a Durban businessman who has borrowed much from Semler for his own context, which also happens to be manufacturing. As he showed me around his factory, spoke of his role and how he saw his responsibilities, I felt a growing excitement – the kind of feeling one gets when discovering hidden treasure. Here was further proof that it *can* be done!

The grace of great things

The nature of leadership

The Sioux believe that children are a gift from God – a gift so sacred, so holy, that they are kept off the ground for the entire first year of their life. The Sioux also believe that children are sent as messengers and so the naming of a child takes place long before birth and is a tribal responsibility. In the process of choosing a name, two questions are asked: Why has this child been sent to us? What message does he or she bring? In fact the Sioux do not even have a word to distinguish a child from an adult. If pressed to describe such a 'little person', they would refer to him or her as a Sacred Being.

I believe this understanding of children to be a great thing. It reminds me of an expression I once came across, 'the grace of great things'.

The grace of great things. It was a phrase that immediately struck a chord within me when I first encountered it – although exactly where and when that was I can't recall. As I have thought about it I have been reminded of how easy it is for us to lose sight of the great things that call us together – the things that call us to pause, to learn, to remember, to serve, to celebrate and to love. To lose sight of the grace that the 'great things' offer can only diminish our community, our relationships, our families at home and at work.

By *great things* is meant the subjects around which a circle of seekers has always gathered – not the so-called experts who study these subjects, not the texts that discuss them, not the theories that explain them, but the actual things themselves. As we gather around and focus on the *subject*, we open ourselves to encounter the grace that is on offer. And as we do so, it evokes from us the courage, security and strength to:

- Explore diversity
- Embrace ambiguity
- Welcome creative conflict
- Practise honesty
- Experience humility
- Discover freedom
- Gift others with space to explore, discover and learn for themselves

It is when these great things lose their gravitational pull on our lives that we can so easily lose our way with others and even with ourselves. We become susceptible to posturing, narcissism and arrogance – in our ways, our experience, our thinking. We become experts, believing that we have more to give than to receive and in doing so become closed to learning, exploring and experimenting.

These dangers are realised when we attempt to make the great things the subject of marketing, or majority rule, or box them in either absolutism or relativism. With absolutism we claim to know precisely the nature of great things, so there is no need to continue the dialogue with them, or with each other. The 'experts' possess the facts, and all that remains is for them to transmit those facts to those who do not know them. With relativism, we claim that knowledge depends wholly on where we stand, so we cannot know anything with certainty beyond our personal point of view. Once again there is no need to continue in dialogue with great things or with one another, for what would be the point?

Great things ... sacred beings ... are mysterious by nature. So, too, is the nature of leadership. Understanding and holding our children as sacred beings, as 'great things', as do the Sioux, is a wise way to approach not only parenthood but leadership too. Respect for the mystery and what it has to teach us is something to be treasured. It is something sacred.

Scribblings ...

You might well be asking just what exactly those 'great things' are? For every person, family, community and business they differ. You will 'find' them as you think about what it is that keeps you together – the things that call you to pause, to learn, to remember, to serve, to celebrate and to love. As you identify those things ... and pause in their presence, you open yourself to the grace available. In a coaching relationship with a senior manager I encouraged her to think about, record and reflect on what for her were the 'great things'. I invite you to do the same ...

A letter to Santa

Self-evaluation: the means to enduring effectiveness

I unashamedly love Christmas and all that it brings with it. Deep down I suspect that some mistake was made in the cosmic scheme of things as I would be far better suited to a northern hemisphere Christmas than to our southern beaches, barbecues and sweltering heat as we sing about a one-horse open sleigh being pulled through the snow.

Over the years a Christmas highlight has been that I get to read my children's letters to Santa. One that stands out was penned by Sipho. It read: 'Dear Santa, how are you? This year I have been good and this year I have been bad. I think though that I have been about six-and-half out of ten good.'

A self-evaluated pass!

Setting goals and undertaking evaluations have long been part of the territory of leadership. Sometimes I think elaborate goal setting exercises stem from a deep need to believe that we can be in control of our future.

The reality is that we are not.

Just ask the person who has been diagnosed with cancer, the parent who loses a child through a freak accident, the employee who has been retrenched, or the person whose home is destroyed by a flash flood. Given the pace of change on this ball hung in space that we call home, goals that spell out the future can be obliterated in a matter of seconds, as the events of September 11 should remind us.

Is goal setting the adult version of writing to Santa? Maybe.

Self-evaluation is another matter entirely. I don't believe that personal development can take place without self-awareness. Leadership, so long immune to sound, honest self-evaluation, could be in for a shock following the meltdown of corporate America and the subsequent call to accountability for those in charge.

Leaders who surround themselves with those who are willing to challenge, who ask the tough questions and who build internal mechanisms for rigorous self-scrutiny will be the ones who will experience enduring effectiveness.

Scribblings ...

If you are going to set goals for yourself at least set ones that are holistic in character. Set the kind of goals that will exercise your growth in areas of self-awareness and not merely performance. A starting point would be to ask yourself (and others), what you need to do to be a better person and leader. That in and of itself is a tough ask. However, the things to emerge will provide you with a launch pad for creating activities, and eventually habits, that will serve to develop, refine and grow you as a person.

Dad, what's a virgin?

Leadership and communication

Keegan's birthday. The decision is that he can take a select few to a movie and that mom and dad will act as chauffeurs for the occasion. The select few turn out to be the entire rugby team; well, so it seems. Cars packed to make a sardine tin look like a spacious condo, we set off to see Jim Carey's *Ace Ventura*. Once there and having safely escorted the rugby team into the cinema, the remnants (Tamryn, Sipho and me) decide to watch the movie *Santa Claus* staring Tim Allan. No prizes for noticing which part of the family carries the sensitive, artistic genes. Mom was left to guard the cars.

It is on the way home that the real telling of the tale begins. Movies watched and popcorn eaten, the happy team is back in my car – it seems I have most of the forwards. In the midst of the chaotic din that has me wondering if the monastic vow of silence would have any appeal for little people, Keegan pipes up: 'Dad, what's a virgin?'

Monastic thoughts disappear quicker than you can say 'Augustine of Hippo'. A *what*? Where is Vicky when I need her? (I make a quick mental note to check whether or not I have untied her from the bumper before focusing on the matter at hand.) Should I just play deaf? Perhaps try the old distract and forget tactic or fake an asthma attack? What kind of question is that anyhow? What do they teach these kids at school? What kind of movie was that and why didn't they just come to *Santa Claus* like all sane people?

As these questions race around my head searching for some clue of adult intelligence, a quick glance in my mirror shows a row, well actually two rows, of fully attentive faces and total silence. What wouldn't their teachers give for this moment!

Very coolly, I bypass the cranial chaos and effectively employ the SAGMF (pronounced SAG-MUFPH) tactic. The SAGMF tactic? Sure you know it and I bet you have even used it to good effect yourself. It's the old 'stall and gather more information' ploy. Anyway, I get some garbled story about a white bat *(how should I know? go and see the movie)* which doesn't help me at all. An expectant silence follows, signalling my turn to speak.

No need to worry, I'm not going to tell you what I said (no free sex education here, although should you wish to purchase the video series you can speak to my agent), suffice to say that I thought I did a pretty reasonable job.

Well, I *thought* I did.

A pensive silence follows my last technical but not too graphic point. Keegan then says somewhat dismissively, 'Nah, I must have got the wrong word.'

It turns out that it had something to do with the white virgin bat in the movie and so perhaps using the 'birds and the bees' analogy might have been a better ploy. The other twist to emerge from this tale was the challenge surrounding the parental debrief as they collected their now sex-educated offspring from our house. What to say? What not to say? What would the kids tell them when they asked the standard, 'So how was the party, Champ?' during the drive home.

It wasn't easy!

But nor is communication easy within the context of leadership. The questions of what to say and what not to say are as relevant for leaders as they were for the parental debrief. Despite multitudinous books, seminars and workshops, problems concerning effective communication still exist. However, thanks to the virgin bat I have learnt to:

- Remember who it is that is asking the question
- Ask clarifying questions to align the response with the enquiry
- Be prepared to have to explain more than once – and maybe to a hostile audience
- Check the movie out first, and if I can't, be sure I take and not fetch in the transportation chain!

PS My concerned Editor asked me, 'Why was Vicky left to guard the cars and not go to the movie?' Of course Vicky wasn't *really* left to guard the cars and nor was she tied to the bumper to ensure that she didn't neglect her duty. That's just a bit of poetic licence to colour the story. No, seriously – go ask her yourself.

Scribblings ...

In the same way that communication will replace authority as a way to manage, so will storytelling replace control as a means of leading (in the post-modern context).

Having read this story, my very sharp Editor asked, 'Could you add the type of question in the corporate world that sums up, "Dad, what's a virgin?" ' I told you she was sharp! It is a good question. What is the inevitable, potentially awkward question that at some point every leader gets asked but would perhaps rather not have to answer? What do you think it would be?

My stab at an answer would be: 'Why should we follow/trust you?' ('Can we expect increases next year?' 'What about bonuses this year?' might be more immediate concerns.) Come to think of it, I like the 'virgin' question. It always exists, doesn't always get asked but always requires an answer.

The bomb, the keys and that damn phone

Learning from chaos

It was always going to be a close call. The misplaced keys simply made it impossible … But let me backtrack to the beginning.

It was the beginning of the notorious 'flea season' – that time of the year when the little black pests start to make their presence felt and the 'take no prisoners' war talk amongst the Coats clan reaches a crescendo. The war council met and decided on the tactic of bombing the enemy senseless with highly toxic and deadly effective Doom.

The plan was simple. Get all but one out the house, set the alarm, suck in some air, trigger the bombs and run for the door. After some debate the war council voted Vicky as the person best equipped and most likely to succeed in executing this operation. The unspoken belief was that it had more to do with lung capacity than sprinting prowess. The preparation went like clockwork. The appreciative family were evacuated, Vicky set the alarm, detonated the bombs and started her run. She made it to the front door in what is believed to be record time and was greeted by the cheering clan. Lock the door and let's go!

Lock the door?

The keys had been left inside! In an instant Vicky had spun around and disappeared back into the fog-ridden interior. Could she retrieve the keys before the alarm was activated? Consensus amongst the clan waiting patiently in the fresh morning air was divided but, to a person, there was nothing but admiration and support for the initiative and endeavour on display. 'Awesome' and 'legend' were some of the words used and they were not out of place at this juncture.

We think she would have made it but for the ill-timed phone call.

What proved fatal was the slight hesitation occasioned by the shrill ringing of the phone piercing the poisonous fog. Getting to the phone and beating the alarm was a task that not even Superwoman could possibly hope to pull off. And so chaos erupted. Deadly air, ringing phone, deafening alarm, mom inside and the rest of the family outside. It was a difficult situation, one that saw the early morning promise shrivelling like a prune in a microwave.

Needless to say murky recriminations linger and some are haunted by thoughts of what more could have been done to avert the chaos. Like I said, it was a difficult situation and one that proves that even the best laid plans can go Iraq.

We live in a time of chaos.

In Greek mythology the gods Gaia and Chaos were partners in creation. It is often the destructive energy of chaos that dissolves the past and gives birth to the future. Times of chaos are rich in their potential to bring disaster or opportunity and navigating such times is no easy task for leaders. Scientists tell us that if we concentrate only on individual moments, on fragments of experience, we will see only chaos. However, if we stand back and look at what is taking shape, see the big picture, we can detect order, form and design. The role of leaders is to help organisations see the big picture and be willing to embrace chaos as a means of giving birth to the new.

Chaos is as much a part of leadership as it is of life. Expect it, deal with it, learn from it and work with it. Sometimes, though, it helps to be on the outside rather than on the inside!

Scribblings ...

Most leaders I have chatted to are of the opinion that any move towards a more democratic style of leadership is a sure road to corporate chaos.

And initially at least they may be right. However, biology teaches us that living systems in a chaotic state will self-regulate themselves towards an orderly state as a natural process when given the chance. That is how systems evolve. They need chaos (the generation of information) in order to develop. The leader who keeps a lid on information and thus avoids chaos ultimately does a disservice to those he or she leads and robs the organisation of its natural evolutionary process. Chaos is needed as much as order to produce change. And we know that in today's context companies that don't change become obsolete overnight.

How does one start to move away from this control trap?

Start letting information run rampant throughout your organisation and then be prepared to ride the wave!

And for the best wave riding lessons yet, have a look at Margaret Wheatley's excellent book, *Leadership and the New Science: discovering order in a chaotic world* (Berrett-Koehler, ISBN 1-57675-055-8).

The fundamentals of physics

Trust: the leader's greatest measure

Kids and bikes. Every parent can tell stories about this subject. Recently a friend and former BMX champion excitedly told me about the bike he was choosing for his daughter's third birthday. Detailed explanations were offered about the aerodynamics and styling of the very expensive mode of transportation, none of which I felt would be of any real significance to a three-year-old. Shortly after her birthday I bumped into my friend again and asked about his daughter and her new aerodynamic bike. He looked somewhat shell-shocked. 'Here's the thing,' he said. 'At her party a friend of ours asked her what she wanted for her birthday and she replied, "I wanted panties but *all* I got was a bicycle".'

My advice when it comes to parents and gifts for their kids has always been: go cheap and stay cheap for as long as you can! There will be plenty of years ahead when cheap won't appease the gods and the range of desirables and affordables will be mutually exclusive concepts. Where is the logic in buying an expensive airport toy when hotel soap or an airline snack will do the trick when you return home after a business trip?

I remember an early episode with Tamryn and her bike. She tended to be somewhat kamikaze on the thing and as we live in a house with a driveway that would make Kilimanjaro look flat, I thought it my parental responsibility to educate her about bikes and steep driveways. Wanting to give her an understanding of how this all worked, I instructed her to start at the top of the drive and said that I would position myself at the bottom where I would be sure to stop her. Yes I know, you are beginning to get the picture, but wisdom with hindsight is easy. Even British management guru Charles Handy said that life has to be lived forwards but can only be understood backwards. At the time, though, my plan seemed sound and the timing good especially as the Boss, who no doubt would have exercised her Security Council veto, was out.

Well, come down Tamryn did, demonstrating that wonderful confidence and trust in their parents that children are so apt to display. It really is heartwarming as a parent to be the recipient of such undiluted trust. By the time she reached me I think she was doing around 80 kilometres an hour, her hair streaming behind her, her eyes bright and she was screaming with excitement. I had locked-in my stance and bravely stood my ground. Of course I did my job; I stopped the bike.

It was at this point that I learnt a fundamental law of

physics, one which relates to propulsion, and that is: If two loosely connected objects (Tamryn and bike) are in a state of rapid motion and one of the objects (the bike) is brought to a sudden state of inertia, then the other object (Tamryn), will continue in a state of motion for a time and distance dependent on the initial velocity at which it was propelled.

Amazingly true!

Post-traumatic research led me to believe that the long-term psychological damage would be minimal and memory recall practically non-existent. This has in fact proved to be the case.

Trust is a strange thing. Something that can take so long to develop can be destroyed in a moment. Trust, like authority, has to be earned. It is the glue that keeps relationships and teams together. Basically, trust is a matter of predictability. Trust develops when people are told something will happen, and it does.

In the future relationships will become an increasing measure in determining business success – a core issue, and one that is as tangible and as real as the profit and loss statement. The signs that this is so are unmistakable and it will be the leaders with integrity who will know how best to instil, nurture and trade in trust.

Scribblings …

Trust will be the currency of the relation/connection

economy – the new economy that is rapidly emerging from the current information economy. In an ever-increasingly diverse world, trust is fundamental to the collaborative and cooperative efforts needed to build successful and sustainable enterprises. Don't take for granted that what you value as evidence of trusting relations is the same measure that others around you are using. A good place to start in the process of building trust with your team, suppliers, clients or whoever, is simply to ask them what you would need to do to secure their trust. It really is that simple. And you might be surprised at what you hear.

Of course you then have to go out and do it – to live it. Mistakes will be made, but ones that don't break the trust are easily repaired and can even serve to strengthen and add further resolve to the trust mix.

Want to better understand the importance and practicalities behind the *why* and *how* in developing trusting relationships? Then you need to experience Horse Whispering! 'What has that got to do with building and strengthening relationships amongst my executive team?' I can hear you ask. Hard to explain (or convince) in a few words so perhaps you had better look for yourself (www.tomorrowtoday. biz – then follow the link) to see how a one-day horse whispering experience can make all the difference. In terms of understanding what it will take to lead in a connection economy the horse whispering experience is unparalleled.

As easy as A B C

Questions leaders need to ask themselves

I once wrote a newsletter to friends using each letter of the alphabet to share an item of family news. Here is an extract of two of the news items that appeared under 'V' and 'W' – not easy letters to lead with, I might add:

Vicky: Domestically challenged with clear expansive voice. Works hard but needs lots of sun. Comes complete with three attachments, all of which are fully house-trained. What have you? Phone ...

What should I write here? I cheerfully ask Vicky who enters the room. After she reads the above paragraph (to get the context) I'm afraid I cannot print her reply. She leaves the room and abandons me to further ponder the causal connection between humour, the mysterious nature of women and the likelihood of dinner.

Many have tried to write an ABC to parenting, in much the same way that others have attempted to do so for leadership, seeking a bottled formula that is as easy to apply as cutting oneself shaving, and one which guarantees success.

I usually cringe at both, yet have to concede that there is some benefit to be had in reading such 'how to' literature. But it has been my experience that everyone, parent and leader alike, essentially has to work it out for themselves. If there is to be a starting point, an 'A', then it surely must be the age-old adage, 'know yourself' (Socrates it was who gifted us with this wisdom). To 'know' yourself liberates you to 'be' yourself. Leadership can so easily become like those old distorting mirrors that change you as you stand in front of them. Knowing yourself, your strengths, weaknesses, likings and limitations is the raw material from which authenticity is crafted.

Of course to 'know yourself' is easier said than done, but here are some questions that might assist you on a journey that is as compelling as it is challenging, and one that is certainly not without its rewards:

- With whom or what are you competing?
- How would you like to be remembered?
- What in your life/work makes you feel alive, gives you energy, renews your heart/spirit?
- What in your life/work makes you feel diminished, saps your energy, weighs heavily on your heart/ spirit?
- What is your sense of vocation/calling in life?
- Were you to map your life to this point in time

as a river, what would that river look like? (This question is best answered as a reflective exercise in which you actually take time to draw the river, depicting the rapids, waterfalls, still waters and so on)

- In what ways has your life journey been like receiving a gift?
- In what ways has it been hard work?
- What does God think of you?
- What do you think of yourself?

Sperm and cells

Leading in a connected world

It all started when I was on the phone and in walked not one but two neighbourhood cats. Showing little, well actually no respect, they sauntered over to Tigger's food bowl (that's our feline resident) and began to tuck in. If at this point they had encountered Vicky instead of me, it is quite likely that they would have lost at least one of their nine lives. Naturally, they were immediately and politely escorted out with nothing more than a verbal warning and a solemn reminder as to just how fortunate they had been in their understandable desire to dine out.

That evening during dinner I am telling the family the tale of the two tails when Vicky knowledgeably informs everyone that it was a good thing I showed them the door before they had the opportunity to 'spray everything'. (One too many TV wildlife documentaries, if you ask me.)

'Spray what?' asks an impressionable and wide-eyed Tamryn.

'Semen,' replies the Matriarchal Wise One.

'Seaman?' responds a now bewildered and wonderfully innocent Tamryn. 'What's that?'

At this point, even the previously uninterested Keegan momentarily stops shovelling food down his hatch, whilst I give silent thanks for the conversational restraint that sees me now merely cast in the role of 'best supporting actor' in this sudden twist to the tale. Time stands still, nature holds her breath. Captivated and inquisitive stares lock on to the Wise One like scud missiles on some defenceless target. But before Vicky can confound us yet again with her dazzling insights into the world of cats, out pops the answer from an unlikely three-year-old source: Sipho, somewhat dismissively, replies, 'Why, don't you know? It's a cellphone of course!'

We live in a connected world. Not just a wired world of networked connections, but one that is biologically and fundamentally connected in ways that are at times difficult to fathom and even to believe. The scientific world of quantum physics teaches that we live in a fuzzy world where boundaries can prove to be elusive and seldom mean what we expect them to mean. Continual focus on these boundaries, looking for clear lines between cause and effect can, in the quantum world at least, leave us frustrated and bewildered. It is useful to remember this when attempting to understand organisations and, in particular, communications within these organisations. Much of our conditioning and training has been to view the organisation, the system, as one made up of parts. These parts can be separated, reduced, quantified, measured and replaced. A profound change in sensibility is required – one that moves leaders to pay attention to patterns, directions and atmospheres. Smart leaders are those who are able to recognise and collaborate with the internal rhythm of what is happening.

PS: Of course we all know that tomcats spray urine and not semen to mark their territory – but who would dare contradict the Wise One?

Speaking for God

Leaders who think CEO spells G-O-D

Keegan and Tamryn are playing in the bedroom. I am within earshot and party to the following conversation which has to do with Keegan asking for a turn at whatever it is that Tamryn is doing.

'What does God say?' came Tamryn's response.

'To me or in the Bible?' asks Keegan.

'In the Bible,' replies Tamryn, obviously not willing to trust her brother's personal revelations or status as one who speaks with God.

'God says,' responds our minor prophet, 'you must not fight with people and that you must give your brother a turn.'

'Oh,' is all I hear of Tamryn's response but from the silence that follows I gather that she is fully persuaded about the authenticity of the message and her brother's role as the conduit.

Having a kid who talks with God and through whom God talks can be a tough business. Having a boss who thinks the same can be even tougher.

Gone are the days when CEOs get to play God.

And now could someone please tell them that?

Scribblings ...

Russia's Ivan the Terrible once had an elephant executed. The reason? It 'forgot' to bow down to the Tsar.

A conversation with a blind man

Staying curious rather than certain

Sipho's adoption meant that the lily-white Coats herd now acquired its own resident 'black sheep' – a literal rather than figurative turn of phrase, naturally. Of course Sipho's presence in the family has given us our own unique insights and laughter. And of course there have been a few tears along the way as well.

I remember once asking Sipho what he wanted to be when he grew up. Over the years there have been a variety of answers from doctor to chef, president to Olympic swimmer. The one I remember best was 'Zulu'. Sipho wanted to be a Zulu when he had finished with growing.

There was also the time when we were sitting on the beach together. Looking around he said, 'You know, dad, there are a lot of black people on the beach today.'

On one occasion Vicky was bathing Sipho's brother and sister when Tamryn asked how we were going to tell Sipho that he had a black skin.

Kids see colour, yet somehow they don't.

I remember hearing the following story at a leadership conference during which we were invited to 'tell a story'.

A mother went shopping with her daughter who was about four or five years old at the time. There was a blind man with a white cane in the shop. In a piping voice, the little girl asked why the man had a white stick.

'The man can't see,' said the mom. 'He's blind.'

'Does that mean he can't see anything?' said the daughter in the same penetrate-through-walls voice.

'Yes dear,' her mother replied, 'but keep your voice down.'

By this time the blind man himself decided to answer the child. Bending down to her level, he told her that he had never been able to see because he had been born blind. Undeterred, the little girl asked somewhat incredulously if that meant that he had never seen any colours.

'Yes,' the man responded. By this time, much to the mom's embarrassment, a fair crowd had gathered around to listen to the enchanting conversation taking place.

And then it happened. The bright little person asked if he would like her to explain to him what colours were like.

'Yes please,' said the willing student, a patient smile on his face.

'Well,' began the little girl, 'have you ever been inside where it is nice and cool and then walked outside and felt the sun shining on you, warming your cheeks and face and then slowly warming your whole body?'

'Yes, I have,' answered the blind man.

'Well, that is what yellow is,' said the little teacher.

'Have you ever been to the beach without shoes and had to dance on the sand because it was so hot?'

'Yes, I have done that,' chuckled the student, clearly enjoying the conversation.

'Well, that is what bright red is like.'

Then came the last question. 'Have you run into the sea and felt the cold water on your burning feet?'

'Why yes, of course,' said the blind man.

'Well, then, you know what brilliant blue is like.'

And so it was that a child unravelled the mystery of colour to an unseeing but willing student by some way her senior.

The best leaders are those who are willing to learn from unlikely sources. The tragedy of leadership is that all too often it carries with it the expectation that all learning has already taken place, all expertise is already locked in. The result? Little or no room for questions, explorations and discoveries. Life is much more interesting if it is an ongoing quest for knowledge, if we remain curious rather than certain.

Who will help you to see the colours?

Scribblings ...

One of the tragedies of much of current leadership, influenced as it is by modernity, is the prevailing undertow that leaders cannot be learners. Somehow it seems that once the mantle of leadership is grasped, answers replace questions and certainty replaces doubt. Often this is as much the conditioning of external expectations as it is of internal mindsets and attitudes. Leaders are not permitted to admit that they remain learners and there can be no big red 'L' signalling 'Caution: Learner Leader' pinned to their back. After all, by virtue of the position reflected in their impressive titles, they are expected to have the answers, know the direction and maintain control.

Or so it seems.

Smart leaders are those who understand learning

to be a lifelong process with the responsibility of leadership simply offering even more enhanced growth opportunities. These are the leaders who don't mind the big red 'L' sign and who even place under it yet another sign that asks, 'How is my leading?' Their journey is marked by reflection and searching: reflecting about those who have shaped them and searching for those who will continue to influence them. They are also smart enough to know that in their search they will encounter teachers in the most unlikely places ... a child, a homeless person, the fruit seller, a pensioner, the person who serves them their coffee or washes their car.

And on seeing colour ... During a recent trip to Hawaii (well if you have to work, Hawaii isn't a bad place to do it) where a colleague and I were involved in the Asia Pacific Leadership Program (hosted by the East West Center), one of the participants made this comment: A friend had told her that when she sees her, she doesn't see colour (obviously intended as a compliment). The participant's reply must have startled the friend, but it is something important for leaders to understand, especially if they wish to deal authentically with diversity. She replied: 'Well then, you don't see me.'

Escape from Alcatraz

Leadership's hardest task

I don't know how he did it, but he did.

Already running late, we were rushing to join friends for a social occasion when a distant cry echoed from the smallest room in the house. Keegan had locked himself in the toilet and was trapped like a bug in a jar. After several frantic but futile efforts, the free members of the family resigned themselves to the realisation that we simply weren't cut out for Houdini-type stunts. Another myth shattered, but then again reality has a way of doing that. Some radical innovative initiative was required if Keegan was ever to experience his own long walk to freedom.

At the height of our increasingly desperate endeavours the possibility of leaving him in there and periodically throwing food in through the window became an attractive option. I started to think of all the money I would save, how clean and quiet the house would be when '... Don't just stand there, get my little boy out of that room!' was the sharp and not-to-be-ignored demand that penetrated the fog of my daydreaming.

It was the window that was to provide the breakthrough. By using an assortment of lethal looking weaponry I was eventually able to dismantle what once had been an Alcatraz-type burglar guard, thereby liberating the prisoner. I suspect he had rather enjoyed all the attention and efforts (mainly sound effects) but had the good sense not to show it, playing instead to his relieved mother's emotions rather than to the 'you-would-be-better-off-in-there' expression on my face.

Leaders can often come to believe that isolation and solid boundaries are the best ways to preserve their position and status. However, lessons from the new sciences yield a novel perspective in the seemingly paradoxical relationship between freedom and order.

It would appear that these two forces – freedom and order – for so long placed in opposite corners of the corporate ring, are in fact partners in creating healthy, well-ordered systems. If people are free to make their own decisions, guided by a clear understanding of the organisational core for them to reference, then the whole system develops greater coherence and strength. The organisation becomes less controlling but more orderly. When leaders rely only on control in order to lead they create the very conditions that threaten the organisation's survival.

Scribblings ...

'Only two things are infinite. The universe and human stupidity, and I'm not sure about the former.'

– Albert Einstein

The irrefutable 'Law of Gifts'

The cost of procrastination

The older they are the more expensive they become. It is an irrefutable law of parenting.

I remember the days when I could arrive home after a business trip and any small, inconsequential thing would appease the kids and serve as an 'I'm home' gift. Often these small but important sacrifices were the shampoo from the hotel, some airplane food (now there's an oxymoron of note) or some last minute offering bought at the local shop around the corner. It was during those days that I even believed that it really didn't matter what I brought; what really mattered was the fact that I was home. Whilst I would concede that there *were* such days, the point is that they didn't last long. Soon such gifts didn't appease the gods and the expense of providing different ones often rose in inverse proportion to the size of the object being brought home.

The law or principle at work here is: *the older the kid, the more expensive the appeasement*.

And that reminds me of another sure law of leading people: the longer you ignore a problem that is brought to your attention the deeper it grows. You might choose to do nothing for a while, and there *are* times when that is the smartest non-action to take. But to ignore the problem, to bury your head in the sand and hope it will go away is seldom, if ever, helpful.

Scribblings ...

Sometimes it makes sense to 'do nothing', other than acknowledge that the problem exists. But in a system or environment that expects leaders to solve problems this can be a difficult, if not fatal, tack to follow. The greater the democracy present within a company, the greater the freedom that allows people the space and time to work things out for themselves. There is much to be said for allowing failure and, equally, for ensuring that if people are to fail, they fail quickly so as not to waste resources and money. For action-orientated leaders trusting in process is tough. Getting those who follow to do likewise can be even tougher.

Once upon a time

CEO: The Director of Storytelling

'Once upon a time …'

… Such magical words, spoken often in a home with little people – words that contrive to conjure up all kinds of memories and emotions, unleash expectations and hold promise; words that children instinctively understand and that capture their attention; words that release us to be voyagers to limitless destinations where the imagination is free to roam.

Stories matter. And so do stories about stories.

Stories inform life. They hold us together, and they also keep us apart. We inhabit the great stories of our culture. We live through the stories of our race and place. Our families and our country provide daily examples of this reality. The epic journey towards the birth of a democratic South Africa is surrounded by countless stories. Some are better known than others, but they were stories that converged from diverse places to form a stream that became an irresistible tidal wave, for ever changing the political and social landscape of the 'beloved country'. These were the stories that were told in part through the Truth and Reconciliation Commission, stories that cannot be ignored and will never be forgotten.

Our very realities are organised and maintained through stories. In striving to make sense of life, we face the task of arranging our experiences of events into sequences across time in such a way as to arrive at a coherent account of ourselves and the world around us.

This account is a story.

There is a growing appreciation of the role that 'the story' plays in today's corporate world. Marketing gurus have been quick to understand this reality as they realise that in the future products will increasingly have to appeal to our hearts, not to our heads. They have deliberately fused stories into their products and we can only expect this practice to gain momentum in the future. We can expect the story to become the product. In 1996 Copenhagen Airport sold ice cubes imported from Greenland and with your ice cube you just happened to get a drink. The point of this? Well, the ice cubes were the story: the cubes contained air that predated the pyramids. Think about it: there you were, sitting in an airport lounge, enjoying a drink which contained ice cubes with encapsulated air dating back thousands of years!

It is as we learn to inhabit our own story that authentic personal growth begins to take place. Storytelling becomes the terrain where we are able to discover the roots of our belonging and make better sense of our need for affection and acceptance. As we learn to share our story we discover the means to help ourselves and, with a bit of grace, perhaps others too. We are therefore beginning to learn that storytelling inhabits and belongs at the core of business.

The core of the company, its genetic code, is made accessible through stories. In this regard there is no one more important than the CEO as the 'Director of Storytelling'. In fact *Director of Storytelling* (DOS) might well be tomorrow's new title for those we currently call 'CEO'.

I once met a CEO of a large and reputable financial institution. I had asked to meet with him in order to hear something of his story, but had not used this line of approach in setting up the luncheon. All I did was ask questions. Questions that probed his personal and professional experiences, crisscrossing these boundaries at will. Questions that I suspect he enjoyed answering, and by the time the coffee was served, had yielded a rich harvest of information. At the end of his storytelling I asked him just who else within his organisation had ever heard what he had just told me. It turned out that no one had, either because they hadn't asked (it's not the kind of conversation that many have with their CEOs) or because he was no Jack Welch who wanted the world to know just how good he was at his job. This man was too humble to trumpet his story throughout the offices of his domain.

What a tragedy! Others were the poorer for such non-disclosure. In the future the successful CEO will be the one who is able to tell the stories which reveal themselves as well as the company's core, its values, its DNA. And as the stories are lived well and shared wisely they will inspire, create belonging, foster pride and nurture a perspective and context for information, change and growth.

Best dust off that favourite storybook and begin to reacquaint yourself with the art of storytelling. No longer will it be sufficient only to interpret the financials, write the reports and make those tough decisions!

Scribblings ...

We shall not cease from exploration
And the end of all our exploring,
Will be to arrive where we started
And know the place for the first time.
        – T S Eliot, Four Quartets (Little Gidding)

I know the following exercise as 'The River of Life' but you may have encountered it under a different name. It offers one of the best ways to bring a person's 'story' to the surface. It needs time, lots of time, some materials and an environment where there will be no interruptions. Your next retreat or staff teambuilding venture are possible opportunities to conduct this exercise.

Each person is given a large sheet of paper on which to draw. There should be crayons available, magazines that can be cut up, glue, scissors and anything else that you think would assist the exercise. The task is simple: using whatever materials are provided, draw your life as a river, starting from the source and ending where you find yourself today. Rivers offer lots of creative opportunity for expressing the twists and turns, the rapids, the waterfalls, and the meanderings of your life journey. You will be surprised at how creative people are and how this exercise offers an opportunity to make some sort of sense, and to form a coherent picture, of our journey. Often what has not been included reveals as much as that which does find its way on to the page. People need to be given plenty of time to complete this task, which can be done in a communal setting with pleasant background music.

Once the task has been completed, everyone is given the opportunity to share their 'river' with the group. People often don't think that others will be interested in hearing their story and seldom do they realise just how important telling our story can be for our own benefit. You won't be bored! Amazing stories of courage and joy, struggle and difficulty will shine through. People will connect in ways they never thought possible and the shared story will build the empathy and understanding that are so important in a diverse team.

(And by the way, if you'd like to read more of just how important stories will become in the enduringly successful businesses and products of the future, read Rolf Jensen's book *The Dream Society*, published by McGraw-Hill.)

It's not important

Leadership and integrity

The mobile phone had been stolen. It was the end of the world – well, certainly the end of all meaningful existence.

Replacement costs were high and money in the bank was low. *Hadn't we told him to save for just such a contingency?* was the smug thought of the parents who, of course, had never themselves had to face such a crisis in their distant youth.

Searches to find a suitable replacement took the phoneless one (Keegan), his taxi driver (mother) and perennial passenger (Sipho) to a second-hand shop where you can buy anything from a stuffed parrot to a jet engine. Sure enough, the shop had some mobile phones – but at a price. It was in the car park that the taxi driver noticed an urgent exchange taking place between Phoneless and Sipho. It was clear that there were some serious negotiations taking place of a type that would not have been out of place in a business transaction involving a politician and Al Capone.

Back in the car, as the search for a cheap mobile phone continued, Sipho volunteered the information that made sense of the car park exchange: 'I have offered to act as a loan shark and front Keegan the money for his phone,' he announced. *Just what do they teach these kids at school?* Sipho somehow has always had more money than his older brother, which is remarkable given their respective take home pay packages.

It was then that our new loan shark revealed a fatal flaw in his business knowledge by asking, 'Mom, what is *interest?*'

Faster than an eel in oil, Keegan responded, 'Don't worry Sipho, it's not important.'

It's not important. Being on the level is very important for a leader. Corporate history is littered with accounts of leaders who failed because they told shareholders/ the public/their employees, *'Don't worry, it's not important'.*

- In 1920 Charles Ponzi was imprisoned for defrauding 40 000 people of $15 million through a postal coupons scam.
  Don't worry, it's not important
- In 1929 Albert Wiggin, head of Chase National Bank, cashed in by shorting 42 000 shares of his company stock. Though legal, his trades were

counter to the best interests of his shareholders. His action led to a law being passed to prohibit executives from shorting their own stock.

- In 1938 Richard Whitney, ex New York Stock Exchange president, propped up his liquor business by tapping a fund for widows and orphans of which he was a trustee. He also dipped into a relative's estate. He did three years' time.
- In 1961 executives of General Electric, Westinghouse and other big name companies conspired to serially win bids on federal projects. Seven members of the electrical cartel served time and were among the first to be imprisoned in the seventy-year history of the Sherman Antitrust Act.

Don't worry, it's not important

- In 1962 Billie Sol Estes, a wheeler-dealer out to corner the West Texas fertiliser market, built capital by mortgaging non-existent farm gear. He was jailed for six years. On his release in 1971 he repeated his trick, this time with non-existent oil equipment. He was jailed again in 1979 for tax evasion and did five very existent years behind bars.
- In 1986 Ivan Boesky was nabbed for insider trading and his testimony helped convict Drexel's Michael Milkin for market manipulation. Milkin did two years in prison, Boesky twenty-two months. Drexel died.

Don't worry, it's not important

- In 1997, only months after Cendant was formed by the merger of CUC and HFS, cooked books that created over $500 million in phony profits showed up in CUC's books. Walter Forbes, head of CUC, was indicted on fraud charges.

- In 1998 Al Dunlap became known as 'Chainsaw Al' for his propensity for firing people. He was then axed at Sunbeam for illicitly manufacturing earnings through overstating revenues – booking sales, for example, on grills neither paid for nor shipped.

Don't worry, it's not important

- In 2000 the world's elite were ripped off by years of price-fixing on the part of two reputable auction houses supposed to be bitter competitors, Sothebys and Christies. Sothebys' chairman, Al Taubman, was found guilty of conspiracy.

So, worry, it is important.

In leadership, integrity is everything.

PS I remember once reading that the Latin root for the word *integrity* is *integritas* which, amongst other things, conveys the idea of integration, lack of compartments, harmony between the parts, wholeness. I like that.

(Historical data source: *Fortune*, Europe Edition, March 18, 2002 / # 6 p26)

A lesson from The Velveteen Rabbit

Leadership and authenticity

One of my all-time favourite stories is Margery Williams' *The Velveteen Rabbit*, the enchanting story of how a toy rabbit becomes real. Like most good children's stories, it holds valuable lessons for adults as well.

The story helps us learn that sometimes what we go through for a friend may make us a little worn and torn, but that's what makes the friendship real. Friendship often goes through testing times, but true friendship endures and even grows as a result of the testing.

I had just finished reading *The Velveteen Rabbit* to Keegan and Tamryn when Tamryn jumped up and down and skipped around the room shouting, 'Look, Dad, I'm real too!'

It was at this point that Keegan remarked drily: 'Tamryn, you're *too real*.'

Being *real* as a leader is no easy task. The temptation to mask things supposedly for the benefit of the troops is all too natural a reaction. There even is a certain rationale to it that makes it easy to justify. 'After all,' the rationale goes, 'if I display any kind of vulnerability (realness), I will lose the respect of those I lead.' And whilst it can be argued that there was a time when leaders were not expected to be *real* – and in that context, and for that particular generation, this style was appropriate – this is no longer the case. That stoic, impersonal approach to leadership simply doesn't work for a younger generation whose behaviour is informed by different values and who look for – and expect – different things in today's leaders. In a world which hasn't fully grasped this fundamental shift in expectation, leaders who choose to be *real* often pay a high price. They are removed, ignored, silenced and remain unelected, but their influence and lives somehow still manage to inspire and provide hope for those of us who look for leaders who understand not only themselves but those they lead.

For me, authenticity and leadership should never be mutually exclusive realities.

'What is REAL?' asked the rabbit one day, when they were lying side by side near the nursery fender, before Nana came to tidy the room. 'Does it mean having things that buzz inside you and a stick-out handle?'

'Real isn't how you are made,' said the Skin

Horse. 'It's a thing that happens to you. When a child loves you for a long, long time, not just to play with, but REALLY loves you, then you become Real.'

'Does it hurt?' asked the Rabbit.

'Sometimes,' said the Skin Horse, for he was always truthful. 'When you are Real you don't mind being hurt.'

'Does it happen all at once, like being wound up,' he asked, 'or bit by bit?'

'It doesn't happen all at once,' said the Skin Horse. 'You become. It takes a long time. That is why it doesn't often happen to people who break easily, or have sharp edges, or who have to be carefully kept. Generally, by the time you are Real, most of your hair has been loved off, and your eyes drop out and you get loose in the joints and very shabby. But these things don't matter at all, because once you are Real you can't be ugly, except to people who don't understand.'

Who is the referee?

Leading without a stunt double

Saturday afternoon weddings.

Why is it that weddings always seem to clash with the one sports event that you have been waiting months to attend or watch? And how come this head-on collision between the wedding and the sports event always escapes radar detection until it is too darn late, and how come the wedding always wins?

There is much to be said for someone coming up with 'How to avoid weddings and stay married – 101 Plausible Excuses for sports fanatics'. A sure bet for the best-seller list, by my reckoning.

It was one such occasion. A wedding, the timing of which didn't make sense to me, and made even less sense to a four-year-old Keegan who not only had to give up a soccer match, but had to take a bath and wear clean clothes too. 'Just look at the two of you,' gushed mother who saw this as a decisive moral victory and would see to it that she didn't lose a chance to remind us of this fact.

The church was full and as I looked out across the sea of faces it was clear that I was not alone in my suffering. Men sat sullen and glum whilst the triumphant, smiling faces of the women present dotted pews that I'm sure were once used as torture racks but had been well sanded and varnished to conceal all such evidence. I immediately felt at one with those who had once been stretched and beaten on the very place where I was now sitting. A pleasant fate, I mused to myself, compared to the one I was presently enduring.

The death rattle of the organ sounded and we all stood to watch the bridal party's stately advance down the aisle to the front of the church. The procession was led by the priest who was dressed all in black, his flowing robe sweeping the ground.

'Dad!' cried an excited Keegan in a voice that attracted the attention of every dad within a ten block radius. 'Who's the referee?'

A simple case of mistaken identity, of role confusion. Quite understandable, considering the all-black garb. I would think, however, that a referee would dispense with the candles and incense prior to the game and that the priest would not have yellow and red cards tucked away in his robes. Nonetheless, I can see how the confusion came about.

Of course some might say that a referee is eminently more suitable at the outset of a marriage than a priest, and I concede that they may have a point there, but that is another matter.

I saw a Goldman Sachs advert the other day which read: *You have no stunt double - this is leading*. In a sense, a priest can't stand in for a referee, nor a referee for a priest.

Leadership responsibility requires the removal of stunt doubles from the set. I guess if you can't take the spills and have no stomach for the action, you have no business being a leader.

Scribblings ...

This is one reason why leadership in a connected/ relational economy is so demanding. It demands authenticity and any role acting or stunt doubles will quickly be revealed and discarded. The demand for authenticity is being driven not only by technology but by a new generation (Generation X) who are asking different questions, making different demands and holding different expectations for those in leadership.

Stuck noses

Helping others 'get it'

'Daddy, my nose is stuck,' was the sombre diagnosis from three-year-old Keegan who was playing host to a heavy cold.

I had never before heard it put that way but could certainly identify with the sentiment. After all, who amongst us has not experienced a 'stuck nose'? And a wretched condition it is too.

Somehow finding a fresh way to state an old problem can make all the difference. In a sense it is the prelude to a 'paradigm shift' – a concept that has grown in usage and popularity but one that I suspect is more spoken about than understood, practised or experienced. How we like to cling to well-worn perspectives and attitudes that fit us like comfy old clothes! And even when they are revealed to be outdated, irrelevant and long past the sell-by date, we still hold on tightly, refusing to let go. Perhaps we fear that to surrender such 'garments' would be to lose something of ourselves, something of who we are.

Then someone comes along and tells us that our *nose is stuck* and, *POW*, we get it! We find the will and strength to move on, to change, and to see things differently.

Leaders often are the ones who are able to frame things differently. And by doing so they are the ones who help others 'get it'.

So just how do you go about this? Well, a good place to start is to find someone who will challenge your way of seeing things, your way of doing things – the deviant, the crazy, the fringe – and take them to lunch. Talk to them, ask them questions and listen. Allow their 'difference' to rub off on you.

The world views through which each of us interprets the world around us are as powerful as they are subtle. Often we are not even conscious of the lens through which we look and judge, assuming that our 'sight' is normal and wondering why others can't just be normal like us. An example of this is seeing the 'red' of a Coke can at a depth below 150 feet in the ocean. At that depth red is no longer part of the visible light spectrum. Yet people do see it. And the reason? Such is the power of scripting in their minds that they see the colour associated with the familiar branding. A major task for those in leadership is to begin to develop ways in which to recognise the lens through which we see things.

Scribblings ...

Once whilst I was in Hawaii, I interviewed Professor Nick Barker, a good friend, mentor and the Director of Leadership Education at the East West Center in Honolulu, for our TT.biz 'Resources for Busy Business People'. In answer to the question: 'What would be the advice you would give yourself were you able to go back to the beginning of your career?' Nick said that it would be to remind himself always to work at holding up mirrors that would enable honest reflection. He added that the challenge is not simply to deepen self-awareness and leadership capacity, to learn from failure and success alike, but to continue to learn how to learn. It was a wise answer from someone who is helping to shape leaders throughout the Asia Pacific area.

Reflecting on who we are and what we encounter is the very soil from which meaning, purpose, perspective and motivation grow. It is also a great way to help us understand just how it is we 'see' the world and thereby engage others who offer us a different perspective.

Barrie, a close friend and business partner is some-one who helps others 'get it'. He is often the one in our TomorrowToday.biz team to holler 'my nose is stuck!' and if you were to ask Barrie what he loves about what it is we do, his answer would be: 'Seeing the lights go on for others.' Being instrumental in facilitating it, or simply being present when others have an 'aha' moment, is one of the greatest things in life. It is right up there with stunning sunrises, music that makes the soul dance, the golf ball that stays on the fairway and that extra scoop of chocolate ice cream.

My bag is packed, I'm ready to go

Preparing to leave

The countdown has started. Of course there are many 'countdowns' as kids grow up, but this one is perhaps the biggest whilst they remain under your roof and in your fridge. The one I am referring to, of course, is preparing to leave home. In just a few days Keegan, free at last of school, heads off to the UK for a year. It is something that has become known as a 'gap year'. I have always found the term 'gap year' a strange one as it betrays a mindset towards life that insists that school should be followed immediately by the 'serious stuff' of more study or work. Certainly that was the way it once worked, but for numerous reasons it is no longer the case.

What I am certain of, however, is that when Keegan returns home, things will never be the same. The rules of engagement will be different and he will arrive back having had the itchy-feet seed firmly embedded in his mind, a natural consequence of travel. Keegan's experience will significantly impact on his world view, enlarging, shaping and moulding it as his horizons expand. Also, he will have experienced something at his age that neither of his parents had done. But I am getting ahead of myself.

As parents, we all know this day will come. Along with death, taxes and dead hamsters, it is a certainty. That doesn't make it any easier and somehow I suspect that it is tougher on moms. I guess it represents a significant severing of the emotional umbilical cord that evokes in moms a deep sense of loss. Perhaps this sense of loss is more acute than that experienced by fathers who ready themselves to welcome their sons, boys who have become men, to the bigger world that awaits. Could it be that the role of mothers and fathers at this point undergoes some hard to define shift in which the emphasis passes from the mother to the father – with sons, at least? Maybe.

Then there is the question of whether or not he is pre-pared for all that the outside world will throw at him. All the 'what if' scenarios play themselves out, leaving parents anxious about how well they have done their job and with that 'night before exams' sensation when you realise that what you don't know now, you never will know because it is too late for cramming. There is the realisation that your role as a parent in shaping and moulding this creature who is about to stretch his wings and fly is done. Whether or not this realisation arrives as a head-on collision or as the sum total of several thoughts in this direction, its impact is daunting.

I have made it a habit to give the following advice to new parents: prepare your child for leaving. It seems odd advice to be giving someone whose child is only a couple of days or weeks old, but I believe it is never too early to be planting that message in the soil of parenting. Some have recalled how odd they found the advice at the time, but how it helped to shape their attitudes and behaviour as parents.

Paradoxically, 'preparing to leave' is a pertinent message for every leader from day one. Leaders who fail to do so grow into dictators who cling to power and position because they have nowhere else to go. They become the sort of leaders who resist change and are easily threatened. They usually surround themselves with those who tell them only what they want to hear, or who echo what they themselves hear. They are the kind of leaders who become trapped and snared in holes of their own making. Ask Saddam Hussein.

Former General Electric CEO Jack Welch, when reflecting on his role and influence on the corporate giant, said that these would only become apparent after he had left. He spoke of leaving a legacy. Popular author Scott M Peck summed it up succinctly when he said that the measure of a successful life is to have loved, lived and to leave a legacy. Leaders who understand these imperatives are leaders who, from the moment they are entrusted with the responsibility and gift of leadership, plan to leave. They deliberate about what they will leave behind and then intentionally strike out in that direction. They build environments and teams that will thrive without them and spend their energy developing the human and logistical resources to make this possible.

Such leaders are usually very different from those who fail to follow such a plan. They always seem to have time for others; they have a welcoming manner about them, one that invites connection and conversation; they listen well because they understand that they can learn from anyone and everyone; they ask and invite questions; they leave you feeling buoyed rather than overawed by their importance, agenda and mood. These are the truly great men and women, those leaders who understand that their role is one of preparation and so marshal their energy and resources accordingly. For an example of this we need look no further than Nelson Mandela. I have met the great man and I can attest to the power of his presence because of his embodiment of the above description.

Dare I suggest that if you feel that others around you are so dependent on your presence that preparing to leave seems incomprehensible, then your leadership is heading in the wrong direction?

Prepare to leave. It is good advice for any leader. Is it easy? Of course not, but then who ever said leadership was easy?

Scribblings ...

I know a wise Bishop who, when he turned sixty, announced that he would relinquish his local and national leadership positions with immediate effect.

He told the story of how he had written a letter to himself ten years earlier, when he was fifty. The letter was to be opened and read on the occasion of his sixtieth milestone. The letter revealed his perspective at the age of fifty on senior clergy who had hung on to their own leadership positions long after they should have vacated them. He vowed that he would not fall victim to the same error and wrote that, at sixty, should he find himself in the same position, he would immediately resign. (In fact his letter contained ten reminders to himself, based on his perception and foresight.) This took great courage for no doubt he would have been strongly tempted to listen to those voices from both within and without encouraging him to 'stay a little longer'. Before I wrote this I made contact with him once more to hear the story. He is still actively engaged in his work and without question could still have been in a position of national leadership. Does he, with hindsight, regret the decision he took so many years ago? Absolutely not!

Can I drive, dad?

Leaders and control

Control is a word that is arguably the source of the greatest conflicts, whether you are a leader or a parent.

In the early years of parenting the issue of control is often reminiscent of a 'phony war' – one easily 'won' by the oversized and dominant parent who terminates any debate with the evergreen dictum 'because I said so'. Let's be honest, which one of us has not been the victim of such reasoning, or even used it ourselves when in a state of siege? We place it right up there with the best of the 'lines-I-will-never-say-as-a-parent', only to hear ourselves utter it before the clock chimes thrice.

This phony war serves only as a warning, a prelude if you like, of what is to come during the adolescent years. Sadly it is a war most parents know to be inevitable, yet one for which most are ill prepared. But that is another subject altogether.

We could argue that control is as important a phase of early parenting as it is in the early stages of leadership. And in most cases we would be right. However, what is certain is that unless there is a willingness to relinquish control at an appropriate stage, the results of the real war can be a bloody shambles. Most wars are just that, and in all wars there are casualties on both sides.

For most leaders the notion of relinquishing control is a frightening prospect and one that often makes little sense to them. It seems counter-intuitive to all they have learnt along the rough road to power and position. To relinquish control, or even appear willing to do so, would seem to be a sign of weakness. Another reason leaders resist handing over control is simply because they have been doing whatever it is they do for so long that they just can't adjust to being in the passenger seat. After all, surely their role is to be behind the wheel – the driver, if you like? And of course finding plausible arguments with which to prop up this logic are as plentiful as quills on a porcupine.

This is all well and good, unless you are the parent of a seventeen-year-old.

For parents the issue of control is no more forcibly experienced than when the growing, grunting, noise-generating *Whatever* arrives home triumphantly waving something that some idiot has issued and which now entitles him (or her … in which case ignore the earlier adjectives) to legally reduce you to a gibbering wreck. Of course I am referring to their learner's licence. Life will never be the same from this point and your control over the car keys begins to vaporise like snow in the Sahara. This triumph of the young would have been preceded by a rare phenomenon – a period of self-induced, self-motivated study in order to obtain the licence.

As I experienced the threat to my once-firm grip on *my* car – the fact that it was my new dream car did not make it easier – there were some interesting lessons inviting learning. For one, I was confronted by my own emotions (predominantly that of 'unwillingness') about relinquishing control. Once the pure and entirely understandable instinct for survival diminished in direct proportion to the increasing skill levels of the learner driver, there were often no justifiable reasons for me to not surrender the wheel, yet often I failed to do so. Meeting the perpetual question, 'Can I drive, dad?' with a hasty, non-discernible mumble (proof that some adolescent tendencies have a long shelf-life) constituted a clear '*No*'. Fact is, I wanted to remain in control – determine the route, decide the speed, dictate the events, be the leader.

But the real lesson learnt from this experience was one that had a certain serendipitous quality about it. I discovered that when the learner is entrusted with the opportunity to get behind the wheel, something amazing happens. The learner somehow morphs into the 'leader'. Suddenly, this sullen creature whose two main responses from the passenger side of life have traditionally been a grunt and a *whatever* begins to initiate conversation in a manner to which I am quite unaccustomed.

'How was your day, dad?'

Huh?

'So what do you think about …?' and so on.

I came to realise that this transformation somehow (and the word 'mysteriously' would not be out of place here) seemed to flow from the sense of control that came from being in charge, from being behind the wheel. It was almost as if something more was expected of the one sitting in that position.

I guess this behind-the-wheel transformation should come as no surprise. We have seen it all before in the playgrounds of yesteryear when kids who became King of the Castle were filled with a newfound confidence that allowed them to call others twice their size Dirty Rascals.

The point for leaders is that others may well surprise you when given the opportunity to get behind the wheel. Smart leaders know this and they are inclined to create frequent opportunities in order to make drivers out of learners.

Of course, a white-knuckle *SLOW DOWN* scream is still appropriate every now and then!

Scribblings …

There is a Hebrew proverb which says: 'Do not confine your children to your own learning, for they were born in another time.'

For innovation to flourish, companies need to embrace diversity; and for diversity to thrive, leaders and managers have to learn to relinquish control. I believe this is where the next major shift will occur in leadership as we currently know it. It is a fault-line ready to erupt, heaping havoc on traditional forms of leadership and structures. Giving up control will mean many things for the leader, not least of which is the possibility that they will have to turn over the company to someone who knows less. To allow self-organisation to take place, control has to be surrendered. We delude ourselves if we think that things such as innovation, process and self-organisation can be managed or controlled, yet all these elements are vital to our company DNA if they are to survive the future. In TomorrowToday. biz we have begun using the term 'unmanagement' more and more in reference to these elements. Unlearning much of what we have been taught about leadership will be necessary in order to adapt to the postmodern world in which we live and do business.

Giving up control provides the air for authentic values to grow within an organisation. If values are to be owned and lived by everybody, they need to be grown from the ground up.

You are not alone

Sharing the journey

How often have you heard those in leadership positions utter the mantra, 'It's lonely at the top'? They usually serve it up in a sort of self-congratulatory and somewhat condescending manner that expects no one but themselves to really understand. It is almost as if the mantra is the coded password to an exclusive club that only the members themselves fully comprehend.

That 'the top' should always be a lonely place is an illusion. As a parent, I think I can prove it.

Parties are no problem when the kids are knee-high. In fact I think that often the extravagant early parties are more about the parents than the kids. A kind of 'if Samantha next door had a jumping castle, let's go with helicopter rides' mentality. Talk about pressure! Anyway the point is that throwing parties at this stage of the journey is really to sweat the small stuff.

It is when kids grow up that parties become a challenge. As parents you seldom get to witness them because any self-respecting teenager will see to it that the main event takes place at a time and place where you are not. However, there is good reason to ensure that you occasionally thwart such plans and report for duty when these events take place.

The main purpose in being present at your kid's party is to remind yourself that there are others like your own. For some parents it might even help to see that it is entirely possible that there are some even worse than your own. To discover that you are not alone as you navigate the times of feeling that your offspring are the result of some mutant genetic bungling, is a very reassuring discovery for most parents. It serves instantly to dispel the myth that the issues you are facing as the parent of a teenager are unique. In fact, experience has taught me to be suspicious of any household with teenagers who appear calm, orderly and 'normal'. Either they have done masterful jobs of deception and disguise or have somehow put a tourniquet around the inevitable.

Turbulence, challenge and discomfort are part of the parent-teenage terrain, and don't let anyone tell you they are not. However it is in this environment that new and better ways can be forged, where growth takes place and, above all, you discover that your issues and challenges are not unique. Such a discovery opens the way to learning from others and sharing some of the joys and frustrations that mark the journey of parenthood.

When you feel that you are alone it is easy to act accordingly. Tragically, many leaders do this repeatedly, creating a kind of self-imposed exile. If only they would throw a party they would discover others who share the same responsibilities and tasks. They would hear the stories of other leaders who have met with both success and failure, and learnt from both. They would discover that leadership need not be lonely. It is what you make of it that matters.

Scribblings ...

I remember talking to the CEO of a very successful medium-size business. It had been in the family for several generations and had carved out a unique niche for itself in the business world. He said he had an 'open door' policy, which meant that anyone could come into his office at any time to discuss whatever was on their mind. There were no gaps, no holes ... everybody was contented. Or so he thought. As I drilled down to deeper levels within the company, the picture that emerged was remarkably different from that held by the CEO. People weren't talking (well, at least not to him) and the open door was a deserted pathway. Often leaders assume that if no one is chatting to them then there are no issues to deal with – rather like those homes inhabited by adolescents where everything 'appears normal'. Many leaders assume that the pathway to their desk is an inviting one, but often it is not, something that seems to remain hidden in their blind spot. To become effective leaders we must move away from the 'imaginary' organisation we design and learn to work in the real organisation instead.

When last did one of your staff talk to you – *really* talk to you?

Leaders need to build appropriate networks for themselves, webs of relationships. These need to exist both in and out of the work environment. They become safe places to off-load, share, be vulnerable, ask questions, listen, be accountable, and process who they are and how they lead. Without such networks and relational webs leaders place themselves at even greater risk in an already 'high risk' zone.

The South African, the Australian and the Blonde

The flawed maxim of leadership

Children seldom misquote you. In fact, they more often than not repeat exactly what you shouldn't have said.

In response to the Sunday school (what a terrible name – it should have been ditched decades ago) teacher's question of who in the class would like to stand up and repeat the Bible verse they had learnt, Keegan's hand flashed into the air. Confidently, he took his place in front of his attentive inmates, er … classmates.

'The boy stood on the burning deck,
Whence all but he had fled.
Twit.'

Before any of the wardens could interject, he launched into another 'verse' for his appreciative audience:

'I must go down to the sea again,
to the lonely sea and sky;
Where I left my scants and socks,
I wonder if they are dry?'

By this time the youngest and nimblest of the wardens had reached him and was able to put a stop to any further verses that would poison impressionable young minds. This single act was most likely responsible for keeping Keegan off any Taliban Christian hit list and which meant we have not had to go into the witness protection programme.

This was not an isolated incident, a fact which strengthens my case. During a church family camp to which I happened to be invited there was a concert on the Saturday night. I was sitting next to a couple who proudly informed me that the young boy, no more than seven years old, making his way on to the stage was their son. I sat back, glowing in the reflected glory of the radiant parents who were now telling anyone within earshot that the boy about to ascend the stage was their son. As parents and groupies settled back expectantly, the master of ceremonies announced that the boy would recite several verses from the Bible. With their spontaneous PR exercise to the surrounding community accomplished, you could almost hear the purr of the proud parents who were about to collect on their efforts to instil in their offspring correct moral values through the teaching of biblical verses.

Now I think I have a reasonable grasp of what is and what is not in the Bible but when the lad started with, 'There was a South African, an Australian and a blonde on a train ...' I must confess that my biblical google 'I feel lucky' search drew a blank. It took some time before the proud smile slipped from his parents' faces, paralleled by the smirks that began to appear on the face of an audience that sensed something memorable was about to happen. By this time the young comedian was well into a joke that was certainly not fit for the occasion. As horror gripped the bloodline of two in the audience, the raunchy joke played itself out to an otherwise appreciative, if somewhat shocked crowd. Certainly there was an almost palpable 'thank-goodness-he-is-not-one-of-ours' feeling among many who had witnessed what would no doubt become a tale approaching urban legend proportions.

The earlier PR exercise, which seemed a good idea at the time, had ensured that there was no place to hide and feeble explanations blaming friends, school and Barney were mumbled to anyone who would listen. I still think it was the highlight of what was otherwise a fairly dull event.

Leaders can be sure that at times others will unwittingly (or maybe not) ape both their words and their behaviour. It is part of the responsibility that those in leadership must accept. It goes with the job. Trying the approach of 'do as I say and not as I do' will not work. Unfortunately there are many leaders who live out that flawed maxim, using their position and authority to forge the way rather than bringing alignment between what they say and what they do.

I was once involved in a series of teambuilding workshops spread out over several weeks with a new executive team of a large corporation. During this time a colleague of mine happened to bump into the CEO and one of the team members at the airport. To his amazement, when they boarded the same flight the CEO sat in business class while the team member made his way through to economy class, where my colleague was sitting. That is no way to build a team. Whatever the rationale – and I'm sure there would be some 'logic' to it – that kind of corporate behaviour spotlights the gap between the talk and the action. What amazes me, both in this specific example and in this kind of behaviour in general, is just how oblivious leaders seem to be to the contradiction at work.

Creating and guarding corporate hierarchies is something of the past. The younger generations (Generations X and Y), when they enter the workplace, will neither understand nor respond to such artificial divisions of status. Adjusting to this reality is a challenge to those who maintain them.

Scribblings ...

Closing the gap between what you say you are and what you really are requires consistent feedback and no small amount of emotional maturity and intelligence. All too often the feedback structures we have so meticulously constructed within our corporate environments conspire against the very reason for their existence. As people learn to 'play the game', manipulate the system and hide behind the respective feedback and performance review facades, authentic feedback gets lost – or is simply not heard. When that happens personal and corporate growth is stalled. Perhaps the best way to check how your words match your actions is simply to ask someone ... *really* ask someone. Determine to avoid any knee-jerk defensive response and be ready to hear something you don't necessarily agree with or even like. Therein lies the discovery of the hidden pearl. Treasure it, polish it and turn it into something of beauty. As you do so you can be sure that others will notice, but that is not the reason for doing it, it is merely a by-product of the process.

Looking for answers

Inviting the questions

'But why?' can be two exasperating words, words that chisel away at parental resolve like water dripping on a tin roof. Of course the fact that they are used in a highly concentrated way at around the three-year benchmark makes it even more unfair and harder to endure. But that is the way it is and there is no escaping it.

It was during this period in Keegan's life that I one day strapped him in the back seat of the car and set off at the bidding of Her Master's Voice on some or other errand.

No sooner had we exited the safety of our domain when Keegan, sensing that he was with a less battle-hardened victim, threw the first 'why?' response to some ill-advised comment of mine. Too naïve to recognise what was going on, I responded enthusiastically, inwardly delighted at the promising father-son conversation that was unfolding. Now I have to admit that it wasn't until the third or fourth 'why' that I got the feeling that something was awry, in much the same way, I imagine, that a blind hobbit would feel stumbling into a maze. It was at this point of no return that I made a fatal tactical mistake. I foolishly decided to press on and attempt to exhaust the 'why' storehouse. A silly mistake, I know, but such is the wisdom of hindsight.

The situation became hopeless. Every explanation offered, whether fat or thin, merely served to elicit another 'why?' From the same intelligence that forbids males from asking for directions, I blundered on, determined to stay the course by mumbling mind-numbing monotone explanations.

And then the breakthrough happened.

After yet another hoarse offering from me, an exasperated little voice from the rear seat said, 'Daddy, just say *BECAUSE*, man.'

Of course!

All my explanations and volumes of words had been utterly wasted. All that had been sought from the enquiring mind in the rear seat was an answer that was usually delivered with the air of parental authority reserved for moms. 'Because.' The final word, the word to stop the 'why' rhino dead in its tracks. The consummate explanation and sought-after answer to every 'why' question.

How could I have missed it?

How long had mom known about this and why was such valuable information not shared with allies? But at least now you know. The answer is a simple, but authoritative, 'because'. Use this trump card early and get over the idealistic notion of your role in fostering intellectual enquiry. Leave that to the teachers who are paid to do it.

'Why?' is one of the best questions to be asking in business and specifically of leaders. Ironic, isn't it? We drum it out of our vocabulary only for me to suggest that we relearn and redeploy it as adults. Of course it can be a risky business as not all environments support such a question, and whether or not your particular environment does will soon become apparent. I believe that environments that don't, with the possible exception of the military, will soon no longer be around anyway, so best you look elsewhere before it is too late.

There was a time when the chain-of-command type of leadership was mainstream, and to ask 'why?' of the all-knowing god to whom you answered, would only destine you forever to be the Gollum-grub on ground floor. Those who dared ask questions were marginalised or regarded as disloyal or unmanageable. Trouble-makers, rebels, the round pegs in square holes, the deviants who needed to be avoided or, at worst, fired. Such people tend to find each other and create colonies of their own, mavericks, outcasts, rebels – those who see and do things differently. But they are more often than not the change-agents, those who make a lasting difference. It is people like this who are needed now more than ever.

Some companies still don't get it. They operate like well-oiled machines that, at worst, expend vast amounts of energy eliminating any dissident 'why?' voices or, at best, answer, 'because … that's the way we have always done it'. They often appear to be well-ordered and harmonious companies with their carefully crafted mission statements, purpose statements, core value statements or whatever statements (very few really know the difference here) prominently displayed. They offer their standard explanation, 'But that's our policy, sir', or the wildly creative variable of, 'But that's *not* our policy, Madam', to any customer foolish enough to venture the 'why' question. Should you succeed in getting in behind the first line of defence you simply encounter more of the same, only this time from longer titles with bigger desks and, inevitably, less coherence.

Tomorrow's leaders will need to invite and encourage questions. They will understand that it is through questions that better ways are discovered, that people are challenged and growth happens. The 'why?' question will be regarded as fundamental to their armoury. And they will succeed in unleashing the chaotic forces needed for creativity and innovation to flourish.

Of course there are many other great questions that should be asked and to those who dare to ask them will lie the spoils of war. Do you hear yourself asking the questions, or do you hear yourself responding with 'because'?

The test might come the next time you encounter a three-year-old!

Scribblings ...

I read the other day that asking the 'wrong' questions generates the 'wrong' answers, followed by 'wrong' directions, and risks a mistaken idea of how well the company is doing. Questions bordering on the absurd are more useful. Finding and then learning to ask the 'right' questions is fundamental to both personal and corporate growth. They become the barometer by which real progress can be measured.

The problem is, we seldom ask the right questions, and even less frequently do we want to hear the answers!

Niels Bohr, who explored the world of quantum physics, would preface any introduction of a new concept by saying to his students, 'Every sentence that I utter should not be considered as an assurance but as a question.' He also reportedly made it a dictum that 'No paradox, no progress'.

Perhaps the ability to perceive, to see or think differently is more important than the 'capture of knowledge'.

Pies, profits and Paris

Leadership and dreams

It started out as a pie business during a school entrepreneurs week. The girls were required to work in teams and start some sort of business, the proceeds of which were to be shared with the school. Tamryn, Ronwyn and Jill decided that they would sell pies during the lunch break. It was a simple operation really: order the pies in the morning, have them delivered to the school, sell them at break and bank the money. There were many more creative ideas but none had the legs to outpace the simple pie business which flourished beyond all expectations. Once the week had come to an end the bold entrepreneurs (with the exception of Jill, who was destined to become like Pete Best – the Beatle who quit before Paul, John, Ringo and George went on to rule the world) asked and received permission to continue their business enterprise. The school authorities, unlike most such institutions, decided not to interfere with their education and said yes.

It was during this time that the girls hatched the dream to go to Paris.

Of course any dreamer will understand the attraction of parentless Paris to two fifteen-year-olds. And so it was that the dream provided the energy that fuelled the business. Excel spreadsheets of projected income were produced and the figures displayed provided a resounding, 'Houston, we have go for launch.' Suddenly what had seemed like a mere pipedream was tantalisingly possible. Naturally there were the doubters, the older brother for one. A rash bet was made that would see R100 pass hands on evidence (or not) of the purchase of the airline tickets.

In the early days it was easy to scoff. However it was hard to ignore or dismiss the reaction to any reference to or image of Paris that flickered across the TV screen. The dream was rooting and slowly the bank balance was growing. The quest to accumulate the necessary funds did have its downside. Routine chores that had once been done lovingly (well, OK, let me be honest, those tasks that had required some degree of coercion) now became chargeable. A further example of this changed approach was the occasion when Duncan, an invaluable friend (and not just because of his IT skills, though we all need such friends), was working on Tamryn's computer. 'Duncan,' chirps the Opportunist, 'would you like a pie?' 'Sure … that would be nice, thanks Tamryn,' says the unsuspecting benefactor. Tamryn scratches in her cupboard, locates a day-old pie, heats it up and presents it to Duncan with, 'That will be four rand. I have given you a discount because the pie is a bit old.' Of course the fact that Duncan was working on *her* computer didn't feature in the equation at all!

The trip at this point is still to happen. However the tickets have been purchased and an older brother is R100 poorer. What seemed impossible is now within grasp and parents who had dismissed the idea now have good reason for concern about two sixteen-year-olds let loose in Paris. But knowing Tamryn and Ronwyn, perhaps it is the French who should be doing the worrying!

As I have watched this story unfold I have repeatedly found myself thinking about its many leadership applications.

For one, there is the power of dreams to shape reality. In fact, what better to shape reality than the powerful, irresistible force of a dream? So many people let *reality* shape their reality and they are the ones who, whilst remaining practical, never are able to inspire in the way that the dreamers do. Recently I met a Durban businessman who had dreamt of building his own manufacturing plant. A young architect with whom he had shared his ideas travelled back from New York in order to be the one to design the revolutionary manufacturing plant. The dream to do things differently from industry standards has seen not only a unique manufacturing plant being developed, but with it a management style and practice that deserves a book of its own. And it was a dream which shaped it all.

Smart leaders work at discovering what it is their staff dream about. Smart leaders understand the power of dreams unleashed within their business and do everything within their power to release that potential.

The thing about looking back on dreams once they have become reality is that it is often easy to forget just how 'big' the dream was in its original context. Take, for instance, President J F Kennedy's dream in the early 1960s to send a man to the moon and to bring him back safely before the end of the decade. It was a dream that had 'improbable' and, for some, 'impossible' stamped all over it. Yet it galvanised and inspired an entire nation and captured the imagination of the world. Of course the chief architect of that dream didn't live to see it fulfilled, but this is often the case with dreamers. A case in point is Martin Luther King and his immortal words, 'I have a dream ...' As with Kennedy, King didn't live to see his dream fulfilled, yet his ability to articulate his dream inspired thousands to move society and to change history. There is no shortage of examples of dreamers and their dreams. Unlike Kennedy and King, Nelson Mandela did live to see his dream mature into reality. Much of what we take for granted in today's reality was once the stuff of dreams, nowhere more so than in the realm of technology.

With the advantage of hindsight we sometimes forget the size of the dream, and just how impossible it seemed at the time, and how crazy the dreamer appeared. That ought to encourage us as we entertain 'impossible' dreams and also give us pause before reaching for the delete key and dismissing the dreamer's idea. It could even be argued than unless the dream evokes an initial response of 'you must be crazy' from others, it is too small a dream and one not worth pursuing.

Smart leaders look for the dreamers.

They ask repeatedly 'why not?' and are prepared to run the gauntlet of the pragmatists, the realists, those who speak sense and know better. They create within their environments incubators in which dreams emerge and hothouses in which dreams can grow. They also understand that not all dreams make the hazardous journey to reality and don't let those that don't make it detract from the belief that others can.

Another lesson to emerge from the pie to Paris caper is that not all will stay the course. The pie business started with three entrepreneurs but ended with two. Like the 'forgotten' Beatle, there was the friend who decided to look elsewhere and as a result missed out on the profitable pie business. This is a fact of life and most of those we meet along the way have at least one story of having missed out on the fulfilment of some or other dream that exceeded the limits placed on it. Those who shape the dream need to remember this reality, as do those who 'miss out'.

The journey the dream takes towards reality is fraught with peril. Certainly, it is a journey characterised by hard work, discipline and the need to say *no* to detours and distractions. The Paris dream has meant all of the above. The sacrifice of break time, day in and day out; the need to stick to the budget, and choosing between the expensive skirt or banking the profit have been sources of frustration and temptation. And then there have been the detractors who have dotted the sidelines dismissing the notion with pronouncements of doom. Of course the further one makes it along the road, the fewer the detractors!

Dreams move people and change things.

Perhaps the content of the dream is not all that important; as Joseph of old discovered following his fallout with his brothers over his technicoloured dreamcoat, 'any dream will do'. As a leader you need to ask yourself when last you allowed yourself to dream. When was it that you last found yourself energised and scripted by a dream? The chances are that if you have to retreat into the distant recesses of your memory to recall such a time, then you and those around you are not very inspired. Dreams that become woven into the fabric of daily life have an extraordinary power. Encountering dreamers is to encounter people who leave an indelible imprint on others. You know when you have been in the presence of such folk and, perhaps best of all, they somehow remind one to capture one's own dream.

Pies in our household have become something magical (and somewhat costly!). They have become reminders that we need to dream and then find ways to realise those dreams, no matter what the doubters say.

So how do you find out someone's dream?

Ask them.

What is your dream?

Scribblings ...

In my experience the gap between the respective dreams of leaders and their followers is in reality non-existent. This is usually a surprise to management, especially those who are, for various reasons, disconnected from their workforce. The reality is that we all want the same things: fair compensation for our efforts, loving relationships, a safe and secure home, good health, the opportunity to do right by our children, stimulating work, the opportunity to rest and pursue our hobbies and interests ... you get the point. The problem is that we limit dreams in the workplace only to those which can be seen and measured according to the bottom line, the balance sheet, by profit and loss. All too often those dreams are not owned by the majority for it is not the majority who stand to benefit when they are realised. The discussions that form and shape such dreams are exclusive – something that, more often than not, renders them impotent and devoid of energy and vitality. Alternatively, to dream collectively in the workplace is to invite discussion and conversation; it becomes inclusive and releases a kind of magic that is hard to predict or describe. But it is a kind of magic which is powerful in its transforming potential and end results.

Do you, as a leader, want to create an ownership mentality throughout your staff, have a motivated and dedicated workforce? Then develop a shared dream. It is not that difficult.

PS: Tamryn and Ronwyn have since been to Paris, with all the thrills and spills that international travel evokes. With that now done and dusted, what, you might wonder, is their new dream? To write a book about their experience!

Swimmers take your marks ...

Leaders and training

All three of our kids can swim. Two of them, Tamryn and Sipho, rather well. In fact both have won Victrix/ Victor Ludorum for their aqua efforts and Sipho has gained his provincial colours.

'So what's the big deal?' you ask.

Well, here's the strange thing. All three kids were taught to swim by their mother. Again, you may ask, 'So what?' Well, what if I were to tell you that Vicky can hardly swim herself? Let me qualify 'hardly swim' so that we are clear about what we mean here. 'Hardly' means that Vicky dons water-wings in the bath tub. 'Hardly' means that she can make it across the pool using a stroke that is something between a doggy-paddle and an ostrich attempting take-off. (Actually, it is worse than that but none of us have had the courage to tell her.) 'Hardly' means that Vicky is at risk every time she encounters a deeper than usual puddle.

I think you get my point.

Yet the fact remains that our kids are as at home in the water as they are plundering the fridge. As a result of this amazing non-transference of skill, Vicky and I have spent a great deal of our adult life sitting alongside various pools, whether for training or galas. In fact, I write this while I wait for Sipho to finish training.

It was while watching Sipho at a recent gala that the following thought occurred. The race lasted all of 32 seconds yet had absorbed countless hours in preparation. All that preparation for just 32 seconds! Hardly seemed justified until I saw the grin on his face which indicated a PB – a *personal best* time. The effort put into the training, the length after length, come rain or shine, had reaped its reward.

I think it is a lot like leadership.

Good leaders are made. Their training may or may not be deliberate but somehow they acquire the attitude, emotional intelligence and skills necessary to become effective leaders. Those are things best shaped in training, away from the glare and glamour of race day. Good leaders have had the kind of preparation that enables them to perform at their peak when it matters most. They don't stop training and putting in the time just because they are already champions, in fact they work even harder than before, set new goals, stretch themselves even further and attempt the impossible.

The training routines of true champions may or may not change, but their attitude and dedication towards training, understanding the role it plays in their success, doesn't falter.

So often I have found that leaders, on assuming the role, position and responsibility of leadership, stop training. Somehow they assume that it is no longer necessary to carry on with the training disciplines that saw them achieve their position of responsibility. They stop learning, stop growing and soon their leadership position is something to be defended, guarded, and the rot takes hold.

Asking most leaders what their 'training schedules' look like is to invite quizzical responses covered with a layer of 'but that's a question for aspiring leaders, not for someone like me'. After all, how often does the CEO voluntarily enrol him or herself on training courses, or lead the charge in exploring developmental opportunities? For many leaders these things are not opportunities to be grasped, but rather threats to be avoided.

Champions have to work even harder, remain hungrier and stay more focused and disciplined.

It is no different for effective leaders and the really smart leaders know it. When last did you attend a course, read a book or engage in a conversation with the express purpose of developing, growing, learning?

If you have to think about it for longer than thirty seconds, you're not in training.

Scribblings ...

When the bird and the book disagree, always believe the bird – Birdwatcher's proverb

Knock, knock ... who's there?

Leadership and reciprocity: What goes around comes around

'He should represent South Africa at sleeping,' was the SMS we received from Keegan's host after he had been in the UK for a few days. Any parent of a teenager will know about the amazing capacity for sleep that the average adolescent carries. In fact, it is sure sign that your kids are about to enter the teen phase when they cease to wake with the morning sparrows and bounce around the house when most normal people are sleeping.

When they were small my kids had this annoying habit of asking me if I was awake when clearly I was not. The shut eyes, the rhythmic, almost musical, snoring and occasional dribble should all have provided ample evidence that the current mode was 'sleep'. But not, it seems, to my sleep disruptors!

It got worse when they brought home a wake-up ritual custom-designed to irritate parents. It involved a little fist pummelling my forehead whilst my eyelids were simultaneously yanked open, accompanied by a cheery, *'knock-knock, who's there?'* As unwelcome harsh light penetrated the furthest reaches of my skull, bouncing off the inside of my cranium, my nose was given a wrenching twist (*'turn the key'*), and finally a squashing of my mouth, leaving me looking like an overdone kissing fish, and the words, *'and walk right in'*.

Strangely, Vicky was never subjected to this kind of abuse. I'm not sure what she did, or threatened to do, to be granted such immunity. But whatever it was, I wish I had followed a similar line of action. Having been woken up in this rough manner for several years has left its scars but my therapist, a kindly person, has assured me that in time I will cease to wake up screaming and hiding under my pillow.

Of course when the kids hibernate into the teen sleep pattern it provides a complete reversal of positions and the best opportunity yet for revenge. This, together with 'embarrassment' (something that doesn't take much mastering and can be effortlessly applied), are the two greatest weapons in a parent's armoury. However, just as one begins to utilise the chance for revenge, turning the torturous *knock-knock* manoeuvre on its former perpetrators, mom comes to their defence. 'Shame, leave them, they need their sleep', or, 'Just remember who will be looking after you in your old age', are two of the incomprehensible defence tactics that come to mind. Of course there was also the 'grow-up, you're acting like an imbecile' approach, which oddly enough served to motivate rather than deter. It was sound evidence that I was on the right track in serving my former captors some of their own medicine.

All of which proves that *what goes around, comes around*. Or in the more eloquent words of some ancient wisdom, *you reap what you sow*.

Leaders would do well to remember this intelligence.

God's gift to parents

The critical core of leadership

Adolescence is a tricky period.

It has been described as that period in a young person's life when they refuse to believe that some day they will be as dumb as their parents. As Mark Twain so eloquently put it: *When I was 14, my father was so ignorant I could hardly stand to have him around. When I got to 21, I was astonished at how much he had learnt in seven years.*

It is a time when everything changes and those changes happen not only without warning, but with debilitating speed. It is the Pearl Harbour type assault which devastates our defences and unleashes a mayhem all of its own. Pimples erupt on innocent and unblemished skin, wreaking havoc with social standing and self-image. Body parts operate with a mind of their own. New skills, like shaving, have to be learnt and mastered. Voices go south and consistently function only with alarming inconsistency. Relatives irritate with variations on that annoying stock phrase, 'Gosh, how you've grown.'

The world they have left behind seems too small, yet the world that has dawned doesn't quite fit. It's too old for some, too young for others. The constant feeling of being caught between, of *almost*, but *not quite*. It is a time when adolescents know more than their parents think they do, but are regularly reminded that they know less than they ought. It is a time when boundaries are rearranged and where space (it's *my room,* Dad) clashes head-on with ownership (but it's *my house*).

It is also the time when 'wants' differ markedly from 'needs' and where the former is usually prohibitively expensive. It is a time when what makes perfect sense to the young person remains incomprehensible to their parents, and the converse also holds true.

It is a confusing time and most certainly a frustrating one. It is a time of experimentation and choices. It is a time of transition and contradiction. It is a time of great insecurity. Yet it remains the inescapable stargate though which all must pass on the way to adulthood, whatever that may be.

I once read that adolescence was God's gift to parents.

At the same time as the teenager is encountering this season of confusion and endeavouring to forge his or her own identity, so the parents are encountering their own challenging territory, more usually called 'mid-life crisis'. This, it seems, is no accident of design and for those parents willing to do so there are rich parallels to be explored between the two happenings. Both periods, adolescence and mid-life, offer learning experiences to be entered into, rather than problems that need to be solved. The shared invitation here is that of 'growth'.

A word of caution. A problem could arise if parents think that they have done with 'growing' and fail to engage this period in both their life and that of their teenager, as a learner. They will then run the risk of missing out on the creativity, the energy, the stimulation that is on offer, settling instead for a detached, remote-control type approach that will fail miserably.

And herein lies the point: parents of children encountering adolescence need to master new skills and make other adjustments. It is a common mistake to look for these skills as a sort of off-the-shelf kit, neatly packaged and complete with easy-to-assemble instructions.

Parenting doesn't work like that, and nor does leadership.

Parenting, as with leadership, is about being a person. The tags 'parent' and 'leader' merely denote roles and responsibilities. What both sets of 'followers' want is to see and connect with the person behind the tag. This remains the critical core of parenthood and leadership alike.

Parents who have neglected to gaze inwards and acknowledge the issues that shadow them throughout life's seasonal changes are ill-prepared to serve as reliable guides to their adolescent explorers. It isn't so much about doing and saying the right things as about exploration and growth. It is about choosing to be vulnerable, honest and real. It is the realisation that the internal agenda is more important than the external agenda and dealing with the latter, without paying attention to the former, is like trying to eat an ice cream cone under the unforgiving blaze of the sun on a sweltering day.

Parents and leaders who don't get this waste time and energy on preserving authority and masking appearances. They busy themselves with the unimportant, the non-essentials, denying the cracks that are all too apparent to astute observers around them.

It is a pity – in fact, it is a tragedy – because it could all be so different.

Scribblings ...

Perspective is so important. And nowhere more so than for parents negotiating their children's adolescence, and of course in almost all aspects of leadership.

In 1945 two popular show business figures were denounced in the US Congress for turning the youth into 'juvenile delinquents'. The two offenders? Frank Sinatra and the Lone Ranger! Perspective is important! And sometimes it just takes time.

Fairies and other magical stuff

Seeing the real magic

It was a party.

Not just any party, but a 'fairy party'. The occasion was the fourth birthday of my godchild Jordan. It had been her call and fairy theme it was to be.

Now that was fine, except for the only boyfriend invited to the auspicious occasion.

Fairies and boys aren't usually compatible. However, holding back on the fairy costume was not this young man's style and in he strode, resplendent in his own Tinkerbell outfit to confidently take his place amongst all the other fairies. I think even they recognised something of just how courageous (and risky) this act was, for in time he may live to regret it, given the numerous video cameras present.

It was a fairy party to be proud of and apart from the castle cake that was demolished quicker than one could say 'Genghis Khan', there were wishes to be granted from cake-eating fairies with magic wands. It was during the magical chaos that ensued that I witnessed a special stardust moment involving the young man and Jordan.

The host fairy was sitting on a little chair when our intrepid male fairy decided that he wanted it.

'May I have the chair, please?' he asked, impressing all who witnessed the request with his polite and respectful tone. After all it was the main fairy he was dealing with here, something he was astute enough to recognise. Jordan obligingly got up, gave him the chair and considered who might require further wishes granted. Having walked a few paces with the chair in tow, the young man paused, turned around and said to Jordan, 'Thank you for standing up', then proceeded to make his way to wherever fairies and their chairs go.

It was a wonderful example of child logic translated into action. Almost as if what had impressed him was not the act of surrendering the chair, but the fact that Jordan first had to stand up in order to make it possible. There was the true act to applaud – not the surrender, but the standing.

Leaders in making their 'requests' – something which leaders are apt to do – often fail to recognise the 'standing' that was required to ensure that the request was fulfilled.

Thank you for standing is something that should not be confined to fairy parties but something leaders should get accustomed to saying more often.

And still more about fairies: The Magic Hill

Avoiding the optical illusions

Whilst on the subject of fairies, here is a tale from a recent trip.

They told me it was caused by the fairies who lived under the road. I don't know about you, but I for one don't buy that explanation at all. I mean, everybody knows that fairies don't live under roads. Caused by the fairies, indeed!

The locals call it The Magic Hill and it is tucked away in the picture-postcard countryside of Ireland, a short drive from the town of Dundalk. And believe me, it is magic of an extraordinary kind. First of all, trying to find the magic hill without assistance from local navigators is practically impossible and has even led to some sceptics proclaiming that the location is a myth, likely conjured from having consumed too much Guinness.

But they are wrong. It does exist, I have been there myself and I have the picture to prove it.

The magic lies in the hill itself. It is an innocuous enough looking hill, seemingly no different from the many before it and not distinguished in any remarkable manner from the many that follow. It lies silently in wait for the unsuspecting traveller, revealing its magic only to those who, having reached the summit, are willing to stop and apply the handbrake on the descent. Do that and you will experience the magic.

And what magic it is! For instead of rolling downhill, as dictated by the laws of physics, you will roll uphill instead. 'Roll uphill?' you say. 'Impossible!' And had I not experienced it myself, I would be the first to agree wholeheartedly with you. But there you have it. Just when you expect to begin rolling gently downhill, you start rolling uphill. It is a very strange experience and one created by an optical illusion that would have David Copperfield green with envy. I was told that the explanation (for those who don't have it in them to take on the 'real' explanation of the fairies) is to be found in the slope of the banks surrounding the road on either side which combine to create the optical illusion. Armed with that information, the fairy explanation only seems to gain plausibility in my physics-challenged mind!

As we drove away, bemused by the experience of rolling uphill (only in Ireland, I said to myself), my thoughts

turned to a possible lesson in this for those entrusted
with leadership.

Optical illusions are not limited to the Irish countryside.
Leaders often suffer such illusions themselves, believing
that they are due to roll downhill when in fact they are
rolling uphill. Leaders who become cut off from reliable
feedback are prone to such illusions. Very often their
perception of present reality differs markedly from
that of their employees in general. Hearing both sides
of the story can lead one to think that they come from
different planets rather than inhabit the same building
or factory. How does this happen and what can be done
to avoid it?

Leaders who are insecure or feel themselves under
siege will often surround themselves with those who
are always quick to agree with them at every turn. Such
behaviour might be motivated by fear or the desire to
appease the leader's ego, but both lead to the same
result: a leader who begins to operate in a vacuum,
divorced from reality and accustomed to hearing only
'fair weather' reports. This seldom happens overnight
and is more often than not the result of accumulated
years of this kind of behaviour. It often happens when
leaders become too comfortable, situations become
too predictable and a crusty resistance to change sets
in. Or it can also happen when egos have grown out of
all proportion and become insatiable in their need for
affirmation and servitude. The real killer is the lack of
awareness of this state of affairs; after all, what leader
reading this will readily acknowledge the truth of this
in their particular context? But show this to those
with whom they work and there might well be instant

recognition and assenting, albeit fugitive, nods of the head.

This fatal situation often arises when leaders fail to grasp the principle of synergy or the precept, *the minds of many are better than the mind of one*. They often come from the school that promotes the 'lonely leader' scenario, the leader out ahead of the pack, deciding what is best for those who follow. These industrial-age images of leadership are relics of the past and cannot fit into the ever-changing present and the unfolding future. Yet, frustratingly, they refuse to die and persist in spite of the evidence surrounding them, the magic hills that deceive and entrap the unsuspecting traveller. What is needed are new mindsets, new styles, new analogies and new stories of leadership – stories that can replace the old ones before it is too late. It is a tough ask and I'm not sure it is within the capacity of the majority of leaders to undertake such daring change. It requires an entirely new game plan and, even more importantly, a new belief that this is how the game needs to be played.

However, there are things that can be done to test whether or not this malaise exists and certainly there are things that can be done to initiate an alternative. The test is simple. Create an opportunity for some open discussion and listen, *really listen*, to what is said. To be truthful, this process is not as simple as it sounds but it is do-able. Care needs to be taken to provide the right environment for such a discussion and outside facilitation is often helpful. There are also tools that can be used to generate healthy and authentic dialogue, two of which are known as the 'Soft Shoe Shuffle' and

'Concept Café'. What is then done with the information is as important as the information itself. The process that follows an excavation of this nature needs to be intentional and open. It is in the process that follows that the real work and sweat will start.

There is no formula or 21-easy-steps to navigate what follows. Each situation, each context, will differ, but trusting those present to find what will work and know how best to implement it, are the best navigation beacons one can hope for. There are basically three phases to such a journey: first, the real desire to test for authentic voices and generate open discussion; secondly, the deliberate creation of an environment for this to take place; and thirdly, a commitment to the process and the changes that will follow. It then becomes the stargate to deep change, buy-in, ownership, innovation and resilience – characteristics that any leader dreams of having in the DNA of the company or organisation they lead.

The stuff of fairies? Maybe not, but you'll have to be willing to stop on the magic hill to find out which way you roll.

Switching off the sun

Preparing for the next generation in the workplace

Hannah (the daughter of a colleague) was strapped in her car seat as her parents headed off for a weekend away. Hannah is a bright, engaging two-year-old and no doubt had thought plenty of thoughts from this particular vantage point, one that I might add she was well accustomed too – as are most two-year-olds.

On this particular occasion, bright early morning sunshine streamed in through her window. After a short while, Hannah's voice was heard: 'Mommy.'

'Yes, Hannah.'

'Please can I have the remote control?'

Allow for a quizzical parental pause here, familiar

ground for any parent of a two-year-old.

'Huh? A remote control? What do you want with the remote control, Sausage?' (*Parental term of endearment ... an entire subject of its own!*)

'I need to switch off the sun, it's getting in my eyes.'

Hannah's request reveals a world view that believes that there is a remote control for everything under and including the sun. After all, in Hannah's world there are remote controls for the gates, the garage doors, the car and house alarms, the TV, VCR, DVD/MP3, the satellite dish decoders as well as remote phones, cellphones, mouses (should that be mice?), keyboards, toys and just about anything you can imagine.

The fact of the matter is that Hannah and her next-of-kin generation (Generation X) are highly techno-literate and will expect your company to be so too. If we thought that the Xers pushed the battery in this regard, just wait until Hannah and her generation (Generation Y) hit the office! (For that matter, schools – the playgrounds for Generation Y before they arrive on our doorstep – had also better upgrade quickly.)

During what we have labelled the 'Information Age', there was competitive advantage to be had through the installation of better and smarter IT systems. After all, assuming they were used correctly, they enabled relevant information to get to the surface quicker, resulting in speedy responses and smart strategies. However this advantage all but disappeared as our competitors installed their own hardware, software and other kind of ware, all of which meant that theirs was newer, faster, and cleverer.

The playing fields have been levelled and having smart IT is necessary but no longer sufficient or even impressive. This is tough to hear if you have just spent millions upgrading your IT systems. Understanding and using technology, personally and as a company, is now an essential skill. And don't believe for one minute that old dogs can't learn new tricks! They can and do all the time. Just this morning I heard of an 84-year-old man who had enrolled himself in school to complete his education.

Attracting and retaining the 'bright young things' in business today requires you to have the 'remotes'. It may not be your world, but it is certainly theirs.

Learning from them how to programme the video machine and how to SMS offer immediate home-based lessons and a place to start ... that is, if you can find the damn remote!

(And if you don't have creatures inhabiting your cave who can impart such skills, I would be only too happy to lend you one of mine!)

Scribblings ...

World views are important. We each have our own world view through which we interpret the world around us; it is the lens through which we see. It has been shaped by our values, and it also shapes our values. For leaders who wish to be effective and optimise their diverse workforce, it becomes critical to understand something of the different generational world views, from the 'Silent generation' to the 'Millennial kids'. There are many excellent resources that will help us understand generational theory and how it impacts on us at home and at work. Graeme Codrington and Sue Grant-Marshall's *Mind the Gap* (published by Penguin) is essential reading.

TomorrowToday.biz (www.tomorrowtoday.biz) also has lots of information on the subject as well as offering powerful multi-media presentations that help us to understand the different generations.

Can you come and play?

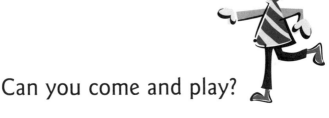

The neglected activity of leaders

Play is important.

For any child, play is serious stuff and central to their daily activities. We have lots of expressions that would underscore the importance of play (*all work and no play makes Johnny a dull boy* is one I recall). But as adults we don't really believe it. At least not if we are to be judged by our responses to, '*Dad, can you come and play?*' Somehow that question always seems to arrive at the most inopportune moment and somehow we repeatedly hear ourselves respond, '*Not right now*', or '*I'm busy but I'll come in a little while*', only never to get around to it. Our schedule always assumes priority over the little people's agenda and timing. Well, *they will learn not to ask when they can see I am busy*, we reason.

A recently overheard conversation between a friend and his three-year-old daughter: '*Dad, you won't work at my party, will you?*' Or the conditioned response closer to home of, '*Dad, I know you will probably say no, but …*' When I hear that precursor it wrenches at my heart because there is no hiding or denying the poor track record that has prompted such an approach.

The next stage is even worse. It is when they don't ask at all. And when you wake up to what you have missed, it is too late and it is the little people who have grown up and are now *too busy*. And there is no going back.

It seems that along the way we are taught that adults don't really play, well, certainly not leaders at any rate. Leadership is serious stuff – there's no denying that. But leaders, more than most, need to play. And I am not just talking about adult play here because we give that important names like vacation, rest, retreat, sport, entertaining clients and so on.

I'm talking about down-to-earth, knee-dirty type play. Engaging with a little person and accepting their invitation to enter their world where you could become anyone and anything. Why, just the other day I became Spiderman. I have always wanted to be Spiderman and for a few special moments I was … until, that is, the game required a tree and the intrepid Spiderman was turned into a weeping willow …

From time to time leaders need to engage in the magical world of make-believe, to indulge in a game of cards or monopoly, to pick up the bat and ball and be the first to holler, 'Let's go play!'

Finding games to play with the little people at home is easy – just let them lead and I bet you will be the first to make the 'time-out' call. In the serious world of corporate life the play is there – it is just that it has been neglected for so long that it might require time and care to restore it to its rightful place.

But don't worry. There will be others who, if asked, will know what to do, and here's a tip: let them decide the play.

Scribblings ...

I was once shown around a very well organised preschool crèche. It catered for a sector of the community that did not have much cash to spare but who were nonetheless fiercely proud of appearances and making the most of what they had. This was reflected in the dress code of the kids who arrived each morning. Each child wore shoes, for to go barefoot was considered a sign of poverty, something that their parents wanted to avoid at all costs. Because of this prevailing social mindset, taking one's shoes off during the morning (and for some the entire day) was considered poor form. If the parents were to arrive and see their kids without shoes they would voice their displeasure to the principal. But here was the problem and dilemma for the principal and her staff. Playing while wearing shoes was problematic. The jungle gym, the sandpit and various other play activities were best done without shoes. In fact, she explained, going barefoot in such instances was important in the kids' development as they learnt to feel different textures with their feet. Yet for the sake of appearances they were denied this opportunity and it seemed that no amount of explanation was going to persuade the parents otherwise.

It occurred to me that many leaders are subjected to the same restrictions as those kids. They are leading with their shoes on when the situation calls for 'barefoot leadership'.

I wonder what those 'shoes' are for you? I also wonder what it would be like for you to try going barefoot for a while?

The gift that wasn't

Leading by doing nothing

It was the kind of gift any twelve-year-old dreams about. In fact Michael had dreamt about it for some time in anticipation of his forthcoming birthday. Michael is the son of good friends and not from our cave, just in case you were wondering.

The gift in question was a radio-controlled car, the control mechanism being a watch that the 'driver' wears. A pretty neat gadget in anyone's toy box!

The toy ER would have called the time of death slightly over an hour after the gift had first been unwrapped. It was a tragic sequence of events.

Water and electronics don't make happy bedfellows and the watch and the swimming pool were no exception. Forgetting the wonder-gadget on his wrist, Michael dived into the inviting blue water on what was a scorcher of a day.

Enough said.

Of course there were the usual recriminations but they soon faded because what had happened had happened. There was no denying it and no use crying over spilt milk. Easy for me to write; I wasn't the one who broke the bank to get the toy.

What was interesting were the 'options' that presented themselves as possible solutions to the 'tragedy'. One that was suggested was to open the gadget, dry the circuitry, reassemble it and take it back to the place of purchase as 'faulty' and in need of replacement.

I have no doubt that for some this course of action would have been rationalised in any number of ways and acted upon.

Some lesson that would have been for a twelve-year-old!

Another option would be to do nothing. Naturally there would be the impulsive voice wanting to deal with the misfortune by simply replacing the drowned gift. After all, it *was* his birthday and this was the main event.

Again, what message would that have sent to Michael?

No doubt the gap left and the trauma surrounding the event will be felt for a long time by all concerned, and especially by the Birthday Boy. In fact, I doubt if he will ever forget his twelfth birthday.

And it is that 'gap' which provides the never-to-be-forgotten lesson. Fill the gap, as empowered parents could, and the value of the lesson is lost.

Do nothing.

This is hard for most leaders, yet it is often the most appropriate course of action even if it is one that runs the risk of being misunderstood. The temptation to intervene is strong. To exercise control, use authority, take action ... to, well, lead.

Semco's Ricardo Semler refers to this passive response as *'active omission'*. Not only does he have a name for it but it is a central theme in his management philosophy and style. Of course there is a unique environment in which *active omission* occurs and to understand this fully you will have to read his book *The Seven Day Weekend*, where he provides several practical examples of just how this works. The case for this course of *in*action is best understood against the backdrop of *process*.

No two processes are alike and leaders (well, smart ones at least) understand the importance of process. It requires toughing out the 'gaps', being patient when things become uncomfortable and avoiding the temptation to give answers, fix, mend or heal.

So take a lesson from a small boy's mishap and the response of his wise parents.

Doing nothing is often the best course of action.

Scribblings ...

Others often refuse leaders the space to do nothing. One reason for this is that it becomes far too threatening because they may be faced with taking responsibility. It is easier to hide behind leaders or blame them when things don't work out. It then always becomes someone else's fault and we deny ourselves and others the space to grow through situations that, in normal circumstances, demand action.

This is a tough thing to understand. You'll need to give it a great deal of thought ... and perhaps read Semler. I wish you luck!

Dear Keegan, as you leave

The Rocket Science of leadership

I wrote a letter and slipped it into Keegan's luggage before he set out on his adventure that would last a year (at least), having finally done with school. It was one I had long been composing in my head and would be the expression of so much that I wanted to say but knew there would be little opportunity to do so in the frantic scramble of the days leading up to his departure.

The last time I wrote such a letter to him was on the occasion of his thirteenth birthday, a habit which I replicated with Tamryn and later with Sipho. Thirteen is a significant marker that indicates a whole new territory about to be explored. I don't know what it is about thirteen, but something confusingly profound happens when that thirteenth switch trips. Somehow your sweet, compliant, obliging child goes to bed the night before and then, *WHAM*, the next morning it is all so different. Anyway, I will leave it to others more clever than I to ponder this mystery.

It was by accident that I stumbled across the letter I wrote when he was thirteen when the more recent letter's trail was still fresh in my mind. As I reread what I had written those many years ago, I was surprised to find that two dominant themes had repeated themselves. The first was encouragement for Keegan to continually grow in his understanding of who he is – which I suggested would be a dynamic, lifelong engagement of a task. In this context I reminded him that who he was would always be more important than what he achieved. The theme is echoed by Meister Eckhart who wrote that 'people should not consider so much what they do, as what they are'.

The second theme was one that I admitted I had been spared for most of my life but that was nonetheless inescapable: that we often learn more from the pain and challenges that life serves us, than we do from experiencing the flip side. The encouragement therefore was not to avoid or shrink from the lessons that arrive in uninviting giftwrap, but rather to accept and embrace the gift of growth that is on offer.

As I thought about letters for auspicious occasions my mind turned to what I would write to you, a leader, if you were about to embark on some or other journey.

It would look something like this.

You may recall that in an earlier series of 'Survivor' one of the participants had the unenviable career description of 'rocket scientist'. 'No, really,' must be something he is used to saying after having had repeatedly to answer the stock question we all get asked: 'So what line of business are you in?' I can only guess that one advantage of being a rocket scientist is that he must get to meet a lot of brain surgeons and helicopter pilots as others try to match his apparent wit and creativity. I mean, come on, how many rocket scientists have you met?

I use the word 'unenviable' because with the job of rocket scientist must come huge expectations, and also some scepticism and no small amount of mystique. Take, for instance, my reaction to the very first challenge the two tribes encountered in their Amazon adventure. I sat there in front of the TV thinking, 'How can the men (the tribes are split according to gender) lose this one? After all there is a rocket scientist on board!' Wrong again. Rocket scientist notwithstanding, the women put one over the men in no uncertain fashion and no one was more surprised than the men. It seems sisters are indeed doing it for themselves!

In some ways the description 'leader' in its various guises – Chief Executive Officer, Managing Director, President, Chairman of the Board, Principal or whatever – runs a similar risk of association to 'rocket scientist' and has to run the same potential gauntlet.

Much is expected of people who carry lofty titles. Both the failures and successes of corporate leaders are glaringly over-exposed in our 'instant-saturated' culture thereby only heightening the scepticism and mystique that surrounds the subject. In pursuit of the elusive holy grail of leadership, an understanding of just what it is and how it is lived, some offer complex explanations that emerge from detailed research. Others would have us believe that effective leadership is as simple as following a tried and tested recipe in much the same way as one would bake apple pie (and more often than not such approaches originate from the land of apple pie). While undoubtedly we can learn from both approaches, the reality is that the art and form of leadership is changing. This should hardly come as a surprise as it doesn't take a rocket scientist (see what I mean about that job?) to work out that the world of business, and therefore the responsibility of leadership, is changing.

Nick Segal, Director of UCT's Graduate School of Business was quoted in the Financial Mail (July 25, 2003) as saying that what is important in the study of leadership is recognising the *style and context* which has an element of cultural specificity. For many leaders navigating the change can be something like attempting to paint a running rhino from a moving vehicle in the African bush. In anyone's language, it is a tough ask.

What, then, are helpful navigational points for leaders negotiating such complex times? Perhaps the best 'navigational points' available are those that would have leaders look both backwards and forwards, embrace both the old and the new in their endeavour to provide authentic leadership.

In 1992 two worlds representing the past and the future, the old and the new, came together in a poignant manner at the equator in the Pacific Ocean. The

Hawaiian people, desperate to reacquaint and connect with their heritage, had constructed a replica of the ancient canoes that had once transported their ancestors in what is known as the Polynesian Triangle, an area spanning some ten million square miles and embracing some of the wildest seas imaginable. Using only the stars and the currents, together with their own considerable affinity for the ocean, these intrepid seamen of old purposefully navigated their canoes over 2000 miles of uncharted open sea between the islands dotted in this vast expanse of ocean. That such voyages were both deliberate and repeated, and not the result of random luck, was something many contemporary anthropologists and historians believed impossible until they were proved wrong by the recreated voyages. The reconstructed replica canoe, christened *Hokule`a* after the star whose scientific name is Arcturus, was completed midst a blaze of publicity in the spring of 1975. It was to become a significant cultural symbol and icon for the Hawaiian people. An article in the *Honolulu Magazine* at this time referred to the *Hokule`a* as a 'space ship of our ancestors'. And so, fast forward to 1992 where Hawaiian astronaut Charles Lacy Veach onboard *Challenger* makes contact from space with those sailing the *Hokule`a* as they both crossed the equator. One orbiting the future, the other navigating the past.

The contrasting and paradoxical image that this picture conjures becomes a guiding metaphor for effective leadership today.

Leaders need to undertake a 'journey of discovery' – a personal *Hokule`a*, in order to discover and connect with the most vital of all leadership ingredients, that of *character*. More so than ever, leadership is about the *who* rather than the *how* and *what*. What matters most is the 'content of character', as Martin Luther King coined it during the cauldron that was the Civil Rights movement in America. Many leaders have spent years constructing impregnable walls around themselves, masking shortcomings, concealing vulnerabilities and in the process becoming strangers even to themselves. For such leaders it may seem that undertaking this inner journey goes against their every survival instinct on which they have relied to keep themselves alive in the shark-infested waters of the corporate world. And in some ways it does.

However, effective leadership demands an authentic understanding of *who we are* and the active dev-elopment of what Daniel Goleman refers to as 'emotional intelligence'. This is not attained by attending a con-ference or reading a book. The journey that is required takes courage and determination and means embarking on a lifelong pursuit. It can take many forms and will certainly at times mean embracing risk and uncertainty. During the course of such a journey feeling lost, exposed and adrift is to be expected. Author Richard Barrett, in an interview with Fast Company, put it this way: *'This is not work for the tentative heart. The benefits of it are immeasurable. Yet it requires personal struggle. Only when you change internally will you see those benefits reflected in the outside world. You have to go through a process, and it is painful. You have to show up fearlessly.'*

The ancient Polynesian adventures were guided

by *Wayfinders*, skilled men to whom the task of navigation, and by implication the lives of their fellow sailors, was entrusted. These Wayfinders navigated by the stars and the currents and trusted their own instincts. Leaders who have not embarked on their own inner journey and who have neglected finding the means by which to undertake such a voyage, cannot serve as trustworthy Wayfinders for others. Finding the constellations and guiding instruments must initially seem difficult, but they are there and each must find his or her own to use and trust. Learning to trust them may prove hard at first, especially in a world where we have been schooled to use detailed maps that offer true north through seven habits, ten easy steps or 21 laws to ensure we find the promised land.

Whilst the *Hokule`a* is a journey of rediscovery, the *Challenger* offers a journey of unique perspective. The *Challenger* enables us to see and understand the world from a whole new perspective and if *Hokule`a* represents the *way of leadership*, then the *Challenger* points to the *task of leadership*.

Effective leadership creates the kind of perspective which enables individuals, companies or even nations to see themselves differently. It is seldom about 'having the right answers', but rather about 'asking the right questions'. This is a shift from many traditional models of corporate leadership. For leaders to gain this kind of perspective and better understand their complex world, they need periodically to turn away from that world and hold it at a distance. It is that discipline which procures the breathing space in which perspective is developed. Without the understanding that comes from such perspective, meaningful change of any kind is impossible. Today, more than ever, leaders are required to break the stranglehold of industrial-age thinking that shackles so many corporations. An entirely new system of thinking is needed, one that realises the rich promise of the emerging relational/connection economy in which the primary focus is people and relationships rather than products and goods. In today's world, leadership is no longer about preserving the status quo (however tempting that may be), keeping others comfortable and ensuring balance. Leaders have to be able to help others cope with an ever-changing world, and not merely survive in such an environment, but learn to thrive in it.

Just as the voyages of the *Hokule`a* and *Challenger* were mysteriously linked, so is the *way of leadership* linked to the *task of leadership*. To attempt one without the other is to tempt fate and endanger others.

What, then, am I saying? Well, to record it in the Captain's Log Book for fellow travellers who may be tempted to think it impossible, the entry under today's date would simply read:

- Effective leadership involves an inner voyage of discovery. It is not without risk or reward, but nor is it optional for those who truly desire to provide authentic leadership.
- Failure to embark on such a journey distorts the necessary perspective that enables a clear understanding of the task of leadership. Without this, change is not possible.
- Effective leaders are contemporary *Wayfinders*.

There can be no greater responsibility.

Bon voyage and stay in touch as much as you are able!

One last scribbling ...

Søren Kierkegaard said, 'To venture causes anxiety, but not to venture is to lose one's self...And to venture in the highest is precisely to be conscious of one's self.'

Acknowledgement:
Stuart Coleman's excellent biography, *Eddie Would Go* (MindRaising Press, Honolulu), is the story of Eddie Aikau, who sacrificed his life for his fellow adventurers on board the *Hokule`a*.